Wire Jewellery

Wire
Jewellery

25 **crochet** and **knit**
wire designs to make

Kate Pullen

GUILD OF
MASTER CRAFTSMAN
PUBLICATIONS

First published 2006 by

Guild of Master Craftsman Publications Ltd

166 High Street, Lewes, East Sussex, BN7 1XU

Text, photographs and jewellery design © Kate Pullen 2006

© in the Work Guild of Master Craftsman Publications Ltd

ISBN-13 978-1-86108-414-9
ISBN-10 1-86108-414-5

Production Manager Hilary MacCallum

Managing Editor Gerrie Purcell

Project Editor Dominique Page

Managing Art Editor Gilda Pacitti

Typefaces: Avant Garde and Typo Upright

Colour reproduction by Wyndeham Graphics
Printed and bound in Singapore by Kyodo

British Cataloguing in Publication Data

A catalogue record of this book is available from
the British Library.

Contents

Introduction

There is something uniquely satisfying about creating a piece of knitted or crocheted wire jewellery. The reason for this is that the process is truly 'hands on'; as you work, the mass of wire and beads that you began with starts to take on a new identity and the end result is a piece that has been designed to your exacting specification.

What's more, while many pay highly for personally designed jewellery, you can make items for yourself, family and friends for very little money. With basic tools, consisting of little more than knitting needles or a crochet hook, intricate and deceptively detailed items of jewellery can be made. Special pieces can be created using precious metals, or fun and funky items can be made from the wide variety of coloured craft wires that are readily available. Beads and gemstones range in price, but there are plenty of stunning options that you will enjoy to work with at the inexpensive end of the spectrum.

The purpose of this book is to explore some basic knitting and crochet techniques and how they adapt to being used with wire. The projects give step-by-step instructions on how to make specific items, but these should really be used as a starting point, as simple adaptations and variations can produce dramatically different items. Not only will a piece of jewellery look completely different if made in silver or shocking pink wire, with glass beads or gemstones, but the items themselves can take on an entirely different form; for instance. earrings can be made into a pendant drop, cuffs into a collar, a tiara into a neckpiece – the possibilities are almost endless…

In addition to providing a good introduction to the combination of wire with these traditional crafts it is also hoped that this book will inspire you to develop new and different ideas with confidence.

NOTES

✖ The techniques that are used in the projects are described on pages 152–170 and should be referred to if you are unfamiliar with any of the instructions. There are also practice exercises on pages 171–172. It is advisable to work through the techniques' instructions and the practice exercises in craft wire before making projects with precious metals.

✖ UK crochet terms have been used. Please see page 175 for US translations.

✖ Wires can be substituted; small increments in size will not affect the appearance of the projects.

✖ The measurements and quantities stated throughout are approximate.

✖ Step-by-step photographs often show items made up in an alternative colour wire to the finished item. This is to ensure that you can clearly see the process being illustrated.

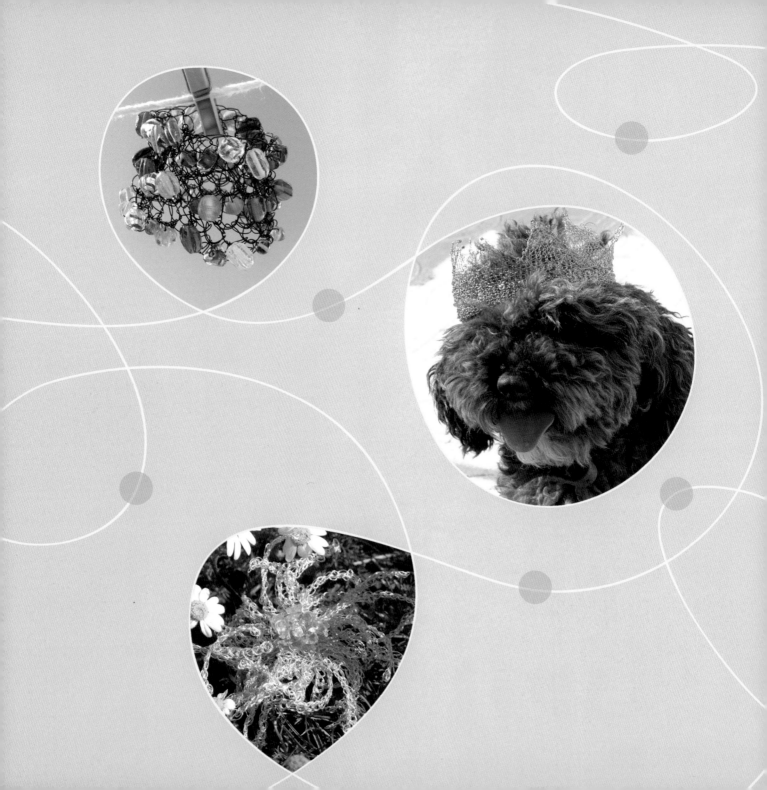

THE PROJECTS

Beaded Crochet Chain

Welcome to the first project in the book. Although it is ideal for beginners, as it allows you to get used to working with wire and beads, the beautiful beaded chain is a versatile piece of jewellery that appeals to all.

The chain is made up into one long length. Once complete it is folded into equal parts and fitted with a necklace finding (see pages 142–145).

To complement the unstructured feel of the neckpiece the beads are dropped into place randomly, with one to three chain stitches between each bead.

HANDY HINT
Thin wire creates the best type of chain; thicker wire is less flexible, resulting in a chain that won't drape around the neck so effectively.

Design Idea

✂ A matching chain could be made for the wrist and worn as a bracelet.

Equipment
2mm (USB-0, UK14) crochet hook
Scissors/wire cutters

Materials
Approximately 300 beads ranging in size from $1/16$–$1/4$in (2–6mm) with a few larger beads added for interest
Approximately 56ft (17m) of 0.2mm (AWG 32, SWG 36) wire
Fastening of your choice

Black craft wire has been used for this necklace and it has been adorned with a rich mix of glass beads. However, it would look equally stunning if made from silver or silver-plated wire and decorated with your choice of gemstones.

The finished length of the chain measures approximately $16^{1}/2$ft (5m). However, it can be lengthened or shortened as required by reducing or increasing the number of beads and stitches.

Beaded Crochet Chain

1 Thread the beads onto the wire (see pages 158 and 169).

2 Make a slip knot (see page 153).

3 Make five chain stitches (see page 154).

4 Start to drop beads randomly between the chain stitches **a**, **b**, leaving a gap of one to three stitches.

5 Continue in this manner until all the beads have been used or until the chain reaches the desired length **c**.

6 Make five chain stitches and then cut the wire, drawing the end through the chain loop to secure. Join the ends by twisting the wires together securely **d** and then neaten the ends (see page 167).

7 Fold the completed beaded chain into equal lengths **e**.

8 Attach the necklace fastener (see page 170) to each end **f** and enjoy!

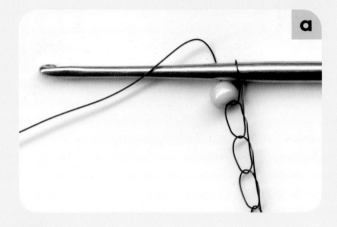

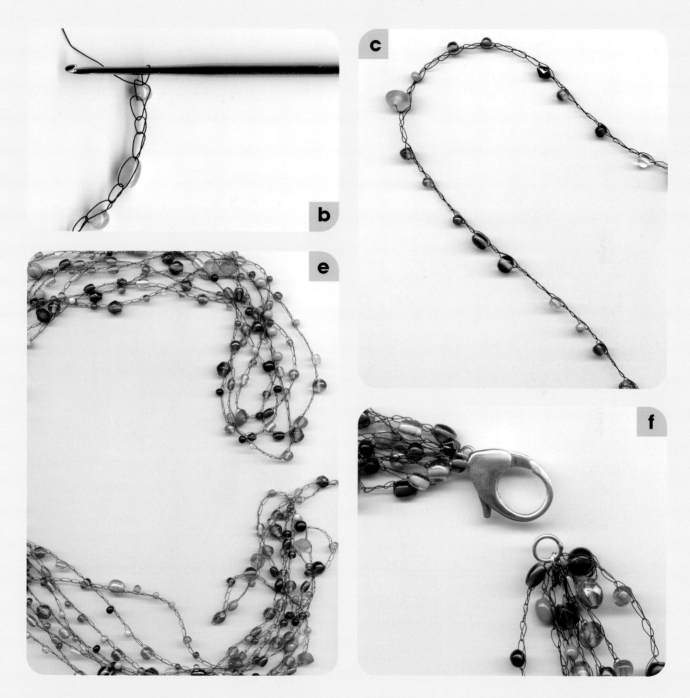

Beaded Crochet Chain

VARIATIONS

This technique is highly adaptable and will give a different effect depending on the materials used.

The peridot chain, pictured below, has been created using fine silver that has been crocheted with a single peridot bead between each stitch.

The small beads are evenly spaced between the stitches, giving a delicate, intricate feel to the piece.

Above This highly individual necklace has a range of different-sized turquoise glass beads stitched randomly into the silver chain.

Right By using Czech crystal beads and red craft wire a very different look is achieved.

Knitted Square Pendant & Brooch

These simple squares are an ideal starting point if you are knitting with wire for the first time. With them you can explore the creation of knitted and folded mesh and how it can be developed to produce a variety of designs.

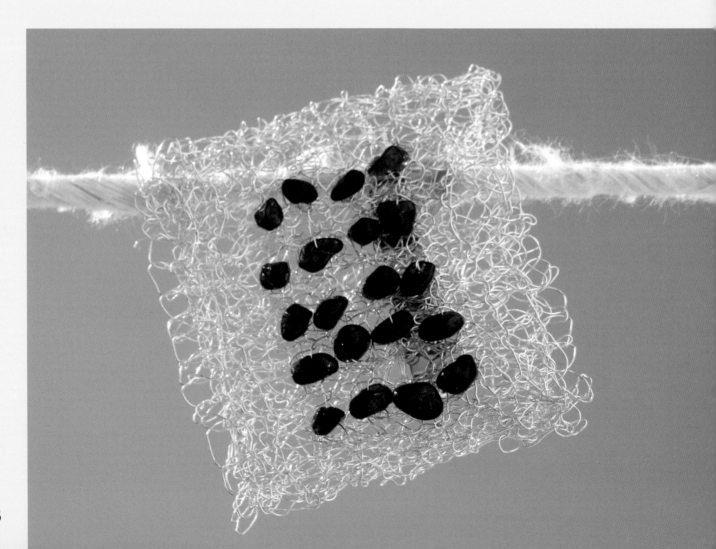

PENDANT (left)

Equipment
2mm (US0, UK14) knitting needles
Scissors/wire cutters

Materials
0.2mm (AWG 32, SWG 36) wire, about 33ft (10m)
Necklet or ribbon as required

BROOCH (facing page)

Equipment
2mm (US0, UK14)) knitting needles
Scissors/wire cutters

Materials
20 beads, approximately $\frac{1}{8}$in (3mm) in size
0.2mm (AWG 32, SWG 36) wire, about 33ft (10m)
Brooch finding

Knitted squares have a highly textured feel due to the layers of knitting. Here they have been made into a pendant and a brooch, but they could very easily be made smaller and used as earrings.

One of the advantages of folded mesh is that it hides any inconsistencies you may have created, allowing you to practise the technique without worrying too much about uniformity.

HANDY HINTS
The 0.2mm (AWG 32, SWG 36) wire that has been used here is very fine but easy to work with. If you wish, a more substantial piece could be achieved by using a thicker gauge.

Remember to cast on and cast off loosely.

1 Cast on (see pages 160 and 162) 16 stitches **a** and knit (see page 163) 45 rows, marking the end of **Rows 15** and **30** – this can be done with a twist of wire **b** .

2 Cast off (see page 165), leaving a long end of approximately 20in (50cm). The mesh will be scrunched up **c** so pull it gently into shape then tidy up the cast-on end (see page 167).

3 Fold the knitted mesh (see page 169) at the points marked **d** .

4 Using the long end of the wire stitch around the folded mesh to hold it in place, leaving a gap to thread the choker.

5 Attach the finding as required (see pages 142–145 and 170). Here a rubber choker has been threaded through one end of the folded square to create a pendant, but you could attach a brooch finding to the back instead if you preferred.

6 Lastly, tie off the wire and tuck it under a layer of the mesh to prevent it scratching the skin.

PENDANT

This project requires you to knit fairly long lengths of mesh. A rectangle is created, which is then folded into three.

Although attractive left plain, the knitted square also lends itself to further decoration – perhaps by stitching in a different-coloured wire (see Crochet Square Brooch on page 28) or by attaching a knitted flower, such as those shown on pages 68–77. It also looks very effective with the addition of beads, as can be seen on page 18 and pages 22–25.

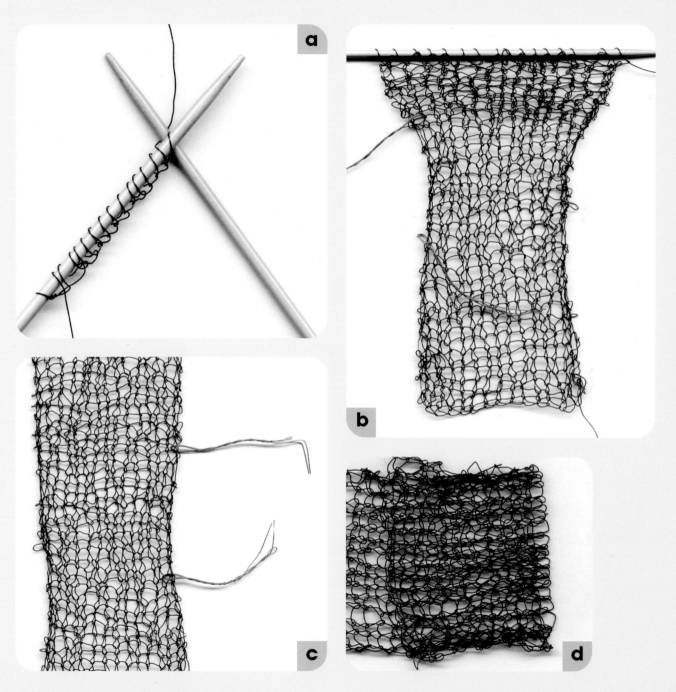

Knitted Square Pendant & Brooch

BROOCH

Using the same method as described in the previous project, beads are now introduced. The beads are pre-strung onto the wire then dropped down into the stitch where required (see page 166). As the beads are knitted into the mesh they will fall to the rear of the work.

This project has been made using tumblechip garnet beads (above) and moonstones (facing page) positioned symmetrically within the mesh.

The mesh measures 16 stitches by 15 rows to allow for the formal placement of the beads, but it can, of course, be made to any size.

1 Thread the 20 beads onto the wire.

2 Cast on (see pages 160 and 162) 16 stitches.

3 Knit (see page 163) four rows.

4 **Row 5** knit four, *drop a bead into place, knit two, * repeat four times, knit two **a**.

5 **Row 6** knit.

6 Repeat **Rows 5** and **6** three times.

7 Knit three rows. It is useful to put a marker at the end of this row – perhaps with a twist of wire.

8 Knit another 15 rows, place a marker and knit another 15 rows.

9 Cast off (see page 165), leaving a long end of wire.

10 Fold the knitted mesh (see page 169) at the marker **b**.

11 Stitch around the edges of the square using the long tail at the end of the cast off **c**.

12 Stitch the brooch fastening into place and tidy up any loose ends (see page 167) **d**.

Knitted Square Pendant & Brooch

VARIATIONS

The knitted square technique, although simple, is extremely versatile and can be a foundation for many different and exciting designs. By varying the thickness of the wire or the number of knitted layers a range of items can be made.

Note: See Crochet Square Brooch & Choker, Variations, pages 32–33, for further suggestions.

Above This small silver wire knitted square has tiny pink crystal beads stitched around the outside. It has been formed into a choker by threading a ribbon through it.

Left Thicker wire has been knitted into a single square and black ribbon threaded through to form a choker. The thick gold wire holds its shape and is not folded.

24

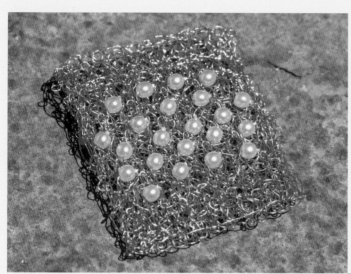

Left Gold-coloured craft wire is interspersed with glass pearl beads. The beads have been spaced at regular intervals to give a uniform pattern to the brooch. Alternative formations Experiment with formations to provide a range of attractive effects.

Right Green craft wire and a selection of green glass beads makes an interesting colour variation. The combination of clear and opaque beads provides additional interest to the brooch. Wide varieties of beads can be combined to give an almost unlimited number of variations.

Knitted Square Pendant & Brooch

Crochet Square Brooch & Choker

Crocheting a thin wire creates a light, flexible mesh that is ideal for practising making wire jewellery. Because the mesh in these projects is folded, any inconsistencies in the stitching can be hidden.

These crocheted squares are ideal for beginners, as they enable you to get used to the feeling of crocheting with wire. Even experienced crocheters will find the feel of wire very different from yarn, and therefore this is a great way to practise while also making lovely items of jewellery.

These are simple projects that are easily adapted. The variations shown here and on pages 32–33, plus the knitted square projects on pages 18–25, should give you some ideas as to how they can be customized to create your own unique items.

Design Ideas

✾ Crochet squares can be made smaller and used as earrings.

✾ Folded mesh is attractive left plain but it can also be made more decorative by inserting beads, as shown below, or by adding an embellishment, such as the crochet wheel pictured opposite.

BROOCH (above)

Equipment

2mm (USB-0, UK 14) crochet hook
Scissors/wire cutters

Materials

0.2mm (AWG 32, SWG 36) wire, about 49ft (15m)
Brooch finding

CHOKER (facing page)

Equipment

2mm (USB-0, UK 14) crochet hook
Scissors/wire cutters

Materials

60 beads, approximately $\frac{1}{8}$in (3mm) in size
0.2mm (AWG 32, SWG 36) wire, about 49ft (15m)
Necklet or ribbon as required

Crochet Square Brooch & Choker

BROOCH

For this project you crochet a rectangle and then fold the work into three. The basic crochet square is left plain but it can have some form of surface decoration if you prefer, such as the crochet wheel shown above (see pages 34–39). The square can easily be adapted to make a choker if required.

The size of the crochet square can be varied either by changing the size of your crochet hook or adjusting the number of stitches used.

1 Make a slip knot chain (see page 154) of 15 stitches. Make a turning chain (see page 154) then turn the work.

2 Crochet 30 rows using double crochet (see page 156) **a** with one turning chain at the start of each new row.

3 Secure the wire, leaving a long end measuring approximately 20in (50cm). Tidy the loose ends (see page 167).

4 Fold the crocheted mesh (see page 169) along **Row 10** and **Row 20 b**.

5 Using the long end of the wire, stitch around the folded mesh to secure it (this is shown in red for illustration purposes) **c**.

6 Fasten the finding as required – perhaps with a standard pin-fitting stitched to the rear of the brooch – either by using the wire that is stitched around the edge of the brooch or by leaving a gap in both sides of the stitching through which to thread a ribbon.

7 Tie off the wire and tuck it under a layer of the crocheted wire mesh to prevent it scratching or irritating the skin.

8 Leave plain or decorate by stitching on a motif, for instance, as shown here **d**.

Crochet Square Brooch & Choker

CHOKER

For this choker, rows of small Czech crystal Bicone beads have been incorporated into the mesh. The beads have been uniformly crocheted along the entire length of every other row, but different effects could be gained by arranging the beads in an alternative pattern – for instance, see the Knitted Square Brooch on pages 22–23 and Variations on pages 24–25.

HANDY HINT
Because the wire is thin, it is best to use small beads so that their weight doesn't pull the mesh out of shape.

1 Thread the 60 beads onto the wire.

2 Make a slip knot (see page 153) then make 15 chain stitch (see page 154). Make a turning chain (see page 154) before the next and every subsequent row then turn the work.

3 **Row 1** double crochet (see page 156).

4 **Row 2** drop a bead into place before each stitch (see page 158) – crocheting 15 beads along the length of the row.

5 **Row 3** double crochet.

6 Repeat **Rows 2** and **3** three times **ⓐ**.

7 **Row 10** double crochet; it is useful to put a marker at the end of this row – perhaps with a twist of wire.

8 Crochet another 10 rows, place a marker and then crochet a further 10 rows.

9 Cut off the wire, leaving a long end, and then draw it through the loop, pulling tight.

10 Fold the crochet mesh (see page 169) at the marker.

11 Stitch around the edges of the square using the long tail at the end of the cast-off (see Brooch, step 5, pages 28–29) and leaving a gap to thread the ribbon through if required.

12 Thread a ribbon or your choice of necklet through one end of the folded square 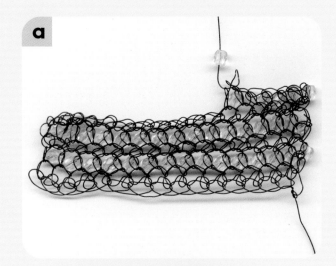.

Crochet Square Brooch & Choker

VARIATIONS

Note: See Knitted Square Pendant & Brooch, Variations, pages 24–25, for further ideas.

Right These earrings are made by folding mesh 'concertina' style several times to form a long, thin drop. They are easily adapted to make longer or shorter drops as required.

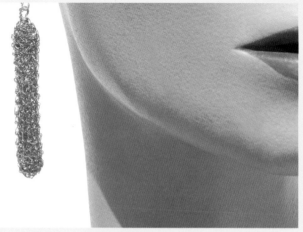

Left Black craft wire and orange crystal beads have been combined to create an unusual brooch.

Below This solid silver brooch is a bit more avant-garde. It was created using a thick wire and a large hook. It was then roughly folded several times to make a substantial brooch.

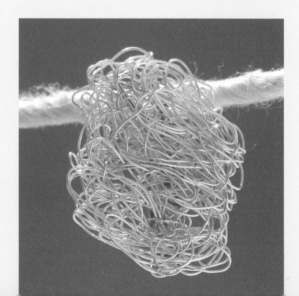

Left This delicate gold collar has been created using a small crochet square, made with a very small crochet hook. A series of crochet chain loops gives detail to the bottom of the finished piece.

Below These matching 'his and hers' rings were made using the technique that is described on the previous pages but the mesh was folded 'concertina' style every row then stitched into a ring. For added decoration small gemstones or crystal beads could be incorporated to form highly individual rings.

Crochet Square Brooch & Choker

Crochet Wheel Earrings

Crochet wheels are simple to make yet very effective. They can be put to a variety of uses, and when combined with beads or gemstones some really elaborate effects can be achieved.

Wheels present an ideal opportunity to get a feel for how basic patterns can be adapted to create a different look, even by simply changing the size of your crochet hook. However, if you do decide to change the hook size, or to use more or fewer stitches, it will alter the amount of wire that is required. So, before working with precious metals it is advisable to make up a sample in copper, or a similar wire, to gauge the amount. An alternative way to calculate the amount required is to measure a length of wire and count how many stitches it produces.

HANDY HINT
Dividing the length of the wire by the number of stitches created will give the length of wire per stitch. Multiply this by the number of stitches required and this will give the approximate total length of wire required. (It is always a good idea to add some extra, though, 'just in case'.)

Design Ideas

⌘ Join two or three wheels together to create dangly earrings.

⌘ Fix one to a hair clip or slide to make a hair drop.

⌘ Create a matching pendant or brooch.

Materials
0.2mm (AWG 32, SWG 36) wire, about 13ft (4m)
Ear wires
36 beads or gemstones

Equipment
2mm (USB-0, UK14) crochet hook
Scissors/wire cutters

For the earrings pictured on the facing page gemstone chip beads were used, with one placed at the end of each silver spoke. The light blue of the aquamarine complements the silver wire perfectly. On pages 36–37, blue beads have been used to create earrings more suitable for everyday wear.

Crochet Wheel Earrings

1 Thread the beads or stones onto the wire.

2 Make a slip knot (see page 153) and then make four chain (see page 154).

3 Join the chain (see page 154), putting your hook through the first chain stitch, wrapping wire around the hook then drawing it back through the stitch and through the loop on the hook.

4 Make three chain and then drop a bead into place (see page 158) **ⓐ**.

5 Treble crochet (see page 157) through the loop 17 times, dropping a bead into place before each stitch **ⓑ**, **ⓒ**.

6 Join the loop, using the technique in **Step 2** **ⓓ**.

7 Break off the wire and then tidy the ends (see page 167).

8 Use jump rings to attach the findings (see page 142) **ⓔ**, **ⓕ**.

9 Repeat to make the second earring drop.

Crochet Wheel Earrings

VARIATIONS

Using different materials can dramatically change the appearance of the finished item; for instance, coloured wire and brightly coloured beads will give a fun and funky feel, while rose quartz and silver will be more sophisticated.

Above This collar demonstrates how the wheels can be adapted to form other items of jewellery. Here they have been stitched onto a piece of crochet mesh to make an unusual and striking neckpiece.

Left These red 'cherry' earrings are made from coloured wire and glass beads.

Left These green earrings have been made using glass beads which have a more uniform size. The colour of the beads is complemented perfectly by the green wire.

Above By using a much larger hook more lacy earrings or pendants can be made. This 'cobweb' pair was made following the same method but with a 5mm (US H-8, UK6) hook.

Left Here the technique has been used to create rose quartz earrings and a matching pendant.

Crochet Wheel Earrings

Knitted Drop Earrings

Although appearing intricate to make, knitted drops are actually very straightforward and can be made as long or as short as you wish.

The earrings that are shown here are adorned with tumblechip gemstones. One of the joys of using these stones is that each one is slightly different in size, shape and sometimes colour, too. It is the natural features of these stones that can really bring a piece of jewellery to life.

The gauge of wire used for these earrings is 0.2mm (AWG 32, SWG 36), which gives them great flexibility of movement. However, if you wish to experiment then a change in needle size or gauge of wire can completely alter the look and feel of them.

HANDY HINT
If you want to extend or decrease the length of the drop then simply adjust the number of beads accordingly (one bead per stitch on each side of drop); for instance, if you increase the drop by two stitches in length allow four additional beads – two on each side.

Design Ideas

⌘ These earrings can be made without the integral loop and with jump rings attached if required. (It is best to use self-locking jump rings so the thin wire doesn't slip out of the jump ring opening.)

⌘ Using the same technique a longer version would make a delicate collar.

⌘ Knitted drops can be made into pendants.

⌘ Create a more formal appearance by using regular-shaped beads.

Materials per pair
0.2mm (AWG 32, SWG 36) wire, about 13ft (4m)
Ear wires
20 beads or stones per drop

Equipment
2mm (US0, UK14) knitting needles
A small crochet hook
Scissors/wire cutters

Knitted Drop Earrings

These earrings are the perfect accessory for a romantic evening, as rose quartz has historically been recognized as the stone of the heart.

They do not require jump rings, as the design includes an integral loop to fit them to the ear wire.

The earrings measure approximately 2½in (6.5cm) from top to bottom (including the loop) and are ten stitches long. The actual length will depend on your tension and the gemstones used, and can be altered by increasing or reducing the number of stitches. If a specific length is required then it is best to make up a sample piece first.

1 Thread the beads onto the wire. Leaving a 4in (10cm) long tail, cast on ten stitches using the beaded cast-on technique, dropping a bead between each cast-on stitch (see page 166) **ⓐ**.

2 **Row 1**, knit (see page 163).

3 **Row 2**, knit **ⓑ**.

4 Cast off using the beaded cast-off technique, dropping a bead into place between each new cast-off stitch (see page 166) **ⓒ**.

5 Using your crochet hook, make three chain stitch **ⓓ** (see page 154) and then slip stitch (see page 156) into place at the other edge of the drop.

6 Cut the wire about 4in (10cm) from the work and, using this and the cast-on tail, wrap the wire around the chain-stitch loop **ⓔ**. Tidy up the ends

7 To complete the earring, attach an ear wire (see pages 144 and 170) **ⓕ**.

8 Repeat for the second earring.

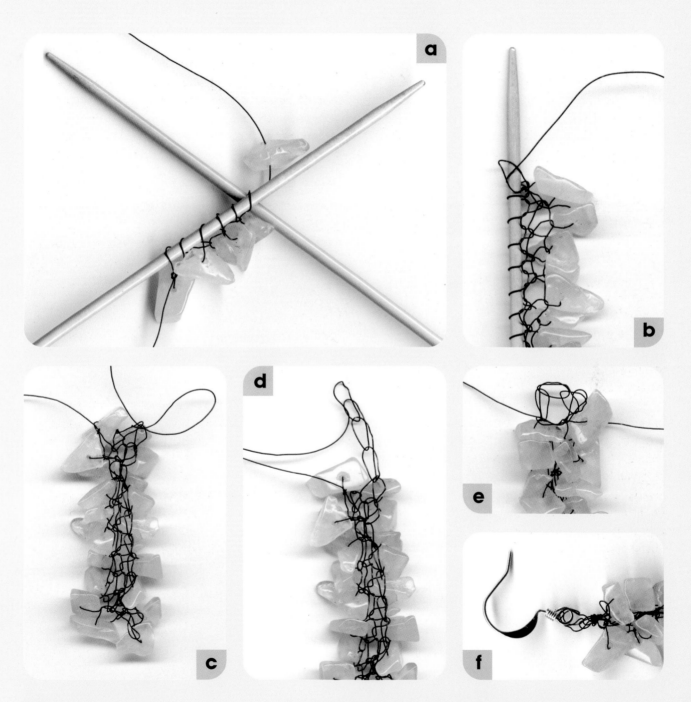

Knitted Drop Earrings

VARIATIONS

For alternative effects, try using different stones or working with coloured enamelled wire and beads. Thinner or thicker needles will also provide either a denser or looser mesh in which to hold the stones.

Below The beautiful aquamarine set on the left was knitted using a pair of 2mm (US0, UK14) needles with a drop of 14 stitches. They look slightly more delicate and formal than the rose quartz pair on the right.

Above These earrings have been made using blue sodalite beads. They are as suitable for daywear as they are for eveningwear.

Knitted Drop Earrings

Bejewelled Crochet Cuff

This is a simple project, but the combination of thicker wire and larger beads is extremely striking.

This crochet cuff is made with a fairly thick grade of wire, which holds its shape well. It is designed to slip over the wrist and be worn like a bangle. The thicker grade of wire means that heavier beads can be incorporated without risking pulling the finished item out of shape.

Equipment
6mm (USJ-10, UK4) crochet hook
Scissors/wire cutters

Materials
0.5mm (AWG 24, SWG 25) wire, about 39ft (12m), depending on size
60 glass beads ranging in size from $1/4$–$5/8$in (6–16mm)

The cuff is crocheted into a flat piece then stitched together at the end. The stitches are hidden inside the beads.

The finished cuff measures approximately 8in (20cm) long and 2in (5.5cm) wide, depending on the tension. To alter the length of the cuff simply adjust the number of stitches used; for instance, to make the cuff 6in (15cm) long, use 16 stitches, or the number required to achieve this if crocheting at a different tension. An alternative grade of wire and use of a different-sized crochet hook will also affect the size.

Bejewelled Crochet Cuff

1 Thread the beads onto the wire, make a slip knot (see page 153) then make a chain of 20 stitches, or the number required to make the desired finished length, plus one turning chain (see page 154) 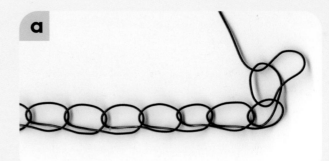.

2 Turn the work and, dropping a bead into place before each stitch (see page 158), make a row of double crochet (see page 156).

3 Make a turning chain, turn the work then return a row in double crochet.

4 Make a turning chain, turn the work and, dropping a bead into place before each new stitch, make a row of double crochet **b**.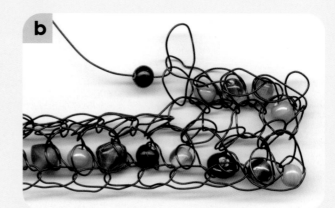

5 Repeat **Steps 3** and **4**, depending on the width that is required.

6 Stitch the ends together (shown in green) to form a bangle shape **c** then gently pull the item into shape if necessary.

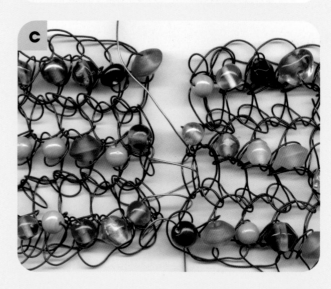

VARIATIONS

This bangle could be made thicker or thinner by crocheting more or fewer rows. Also, by changing the beads, or simply leaving the bangle plain, different effects can be achieved, as shown here.

Right Two rose quartz beads are dropped into each beaded stitch for a highly decorative effect.

Below Simple gold-plated wire shows the pattern of the stitches.

Bejewelled Crochet Cuff

Beaded Knitted Cuff

This pretty, delicate cuff is knitted in a very fine wire, creating a light and lacy mesh that is easy to wear.

The fine wire showcases the lovely stitch detail and the rows of tiny beads provide a uniform structure. Small grey Czech crystal Bicone beads have been used, but any small beads would work just as well (because of the lightweight nature of this cuff it is best to use small beads so that you don't risk pulling the mesh out of shape).

Equipment
2mm (US0, UK14) knitting needles
Scissors/wire cutters

Materials
143 beads, approximately ⅛in (3mm) in size
0.2mm (AWG 32, SWG 36) wire, about 33ft (10m)
Bracelet fastening

Czech crystal Bicone beads have been used to create rows among the beaded mesh. They are positioned at every fourth row. The first and last stitch in each beaded row has been left plain to ensure a neat edge to the work.

As the cuff is lightweight, a 'hem' has been made at either end to provide additional support and enable the fastening to be attached. The hem is formed by folding over the first and last unbeaded sections of the cuff and then stitching them in place. A thicker undercuff could be knitted in a heavier grade of wire and stitched to the finished item for added support if required.

Although it has been designed to fit snugly around the wrist, this cuff can be made looser by knitting more rows. It can also be made wider or narrower by adjusting the number of stitches used.

Beaded Knitted Cuff

1 Thread the beads onto the wire.

2 Cast on 15 stitches.

3 Knit eight rows .

4 **Row 9** knit one, drop a bead into each of the next 13 stitches, then knit the last stitch without a bead.

5 **Rows 10, 11** and **12** knit.

6 Repeat **Rows 9, 10, 11** and **12** 11 times or until cuff reaches desired length **b**.

7 Knit five rows. It is useful to put a marker at the end of the last row – perhaps with a twist of wire.

8 Cast off, leaving a long end of wire **c**, and pull gently into shape.

9 Fold the knitted mesh at the fourth row in from each end **d**.

10 Stitch around the folded edges (shown in grey wire) **e**.

11 Stitch the bracelet fastening into place **f**.

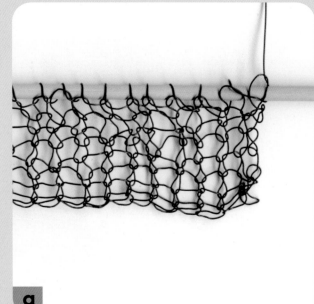

a

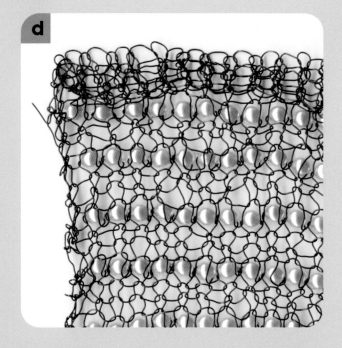

d

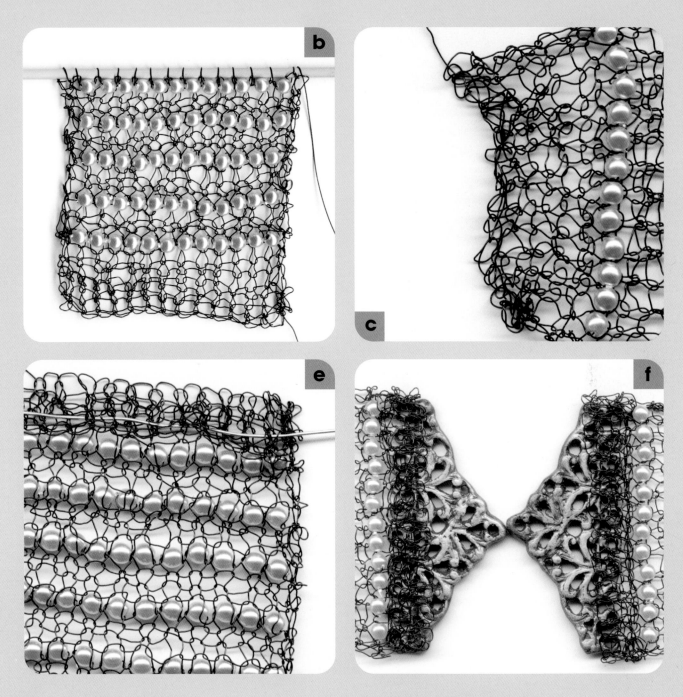

Beaded Knitted Cuff

VARIATIONS

The basic technique of knitting or crocheting a strip of mesh lends itself to being adapted in a way that is unique to the maker. Varying the pattern of beads or stones, or the thickness of the cuff, creates a whole new range of possibilities.

Right Using a solid silver wire of a thicker gauge with 'teardrop' carnelian beads, this highly unusual cuff shows how materials can be varied to great effect.

Below The rose quartz and silver cuff is knitted using two strands of wire which gives it additional strength, allowing larger beads to be incorporated.

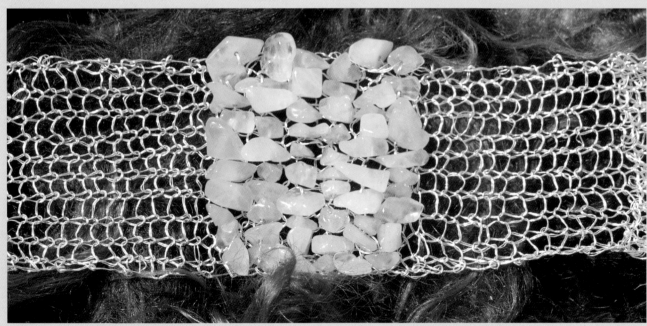

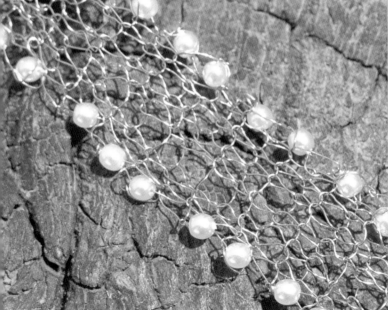

Above left The blue stone cuff has sodalite beads that have been knitted using a thicker wire into every other row to give a complete mesh of stones. Two strands of thinner wire could be used instead.

Above This cuff has been created using tiny peridot beads knitted into every other row using a single strand of silver wire. The beads sit within the stitches, giving a completely different look to the cuff.

Left A thin bracelet has been made using the same technique but knitted over seven stitches, with beads incorporated into only the first and last stitches of every other row.

Beaded Knitted Cuff

Knitted Gauntlet

This cuff is knitted in thick wire, which holds its form and allows the technique of shaping using different-sized needles to be explored.

The gauntlet is designed to curve into the wrist and is laced up with a ribbon. The result is an interesting juxtaposition between the hard, shiny metal and the voluptuous, soft ribbon. It can be worn with the laced fastening facing towards the wrist or outwards. The cuff is shaped using three different-sized needles; the smaller the needle the tighter the stitches become, pulling the centre of the cuff in.

Equipment
6mm (US10, UK4), 4mm (US6, UK8) and 2mm (US0, UK14) knitting needles
Scissors/wire cutters

Materials
0.5mm (AWG 24, SWG 25) wire, about 19$\frac{1}{2}$ft (6m)
Ribbon to fasten

Because the thicker grade of wire holds its form well a traditional cast-on/cast-off technique is not required. Instead, the wire is wrapped around the needle to form the loops using the half-hitch method to cast on (see page 161). To finish, a wire is pulled through the loops at the end, which tightens them to hold their shape. If you prefer, though, a traditional cast-on or cast-off can be used but you must make sure you keep it very loose.

HANDY HINTS
If you find the project hard going with 0.5mm (AWG 24, SWG 25) wire, either knit it in a couple of sittings or use 0.4mm (AWG 26, SWG 27) wire to create a slightly more lightweight version.

Because you are knitting with a thicker grade of wire there will be the temptation to 'tug' the wire around the needle, winding it tightly. Resist. Remember that wire has no 'give' and therefore if it is pulled too tight round the needle it will be extremely unforgiving on your hands. This is particularly important when changing to the larger-sized needles.

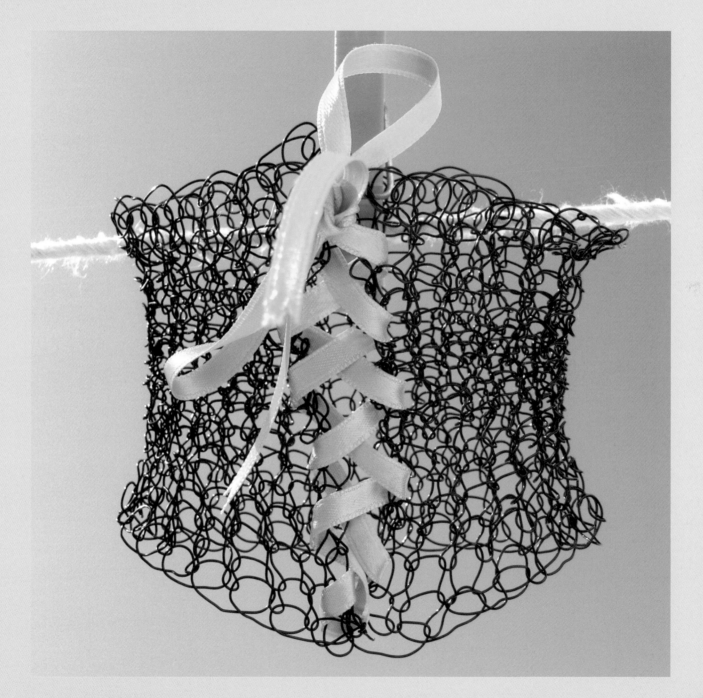

Knitted Gauntlet

1 With 6mm (US10, UK4) needles, cast on 30 stitches using the half-hitch method (see page 161) 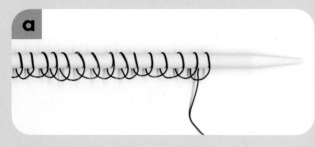.

2 Knit three rows (do not pull the needles too far apart when knitting the first row).

3 Change to 4mm (US6, UK8) needles and knit three rows **b**.

4 Change to 2mm (US0, UK14) needles and knit six rows.

5 Change back to 4mm (US6, UK8) needles and knit three more rows.

6 Change back to 6mm (US10, UK4) needles and knit a further three rows **c**.

7 To cast off, cut the wire, leaving a tail about twice the length of the edge of the gauntlet. Wrap the wire around each stitch to the end of the work then tidy the loose end by working it back into the stitches **d**.

8 Pull the gauntlet into shape.

9 To fasten, thread the gauntlet with a ribbon. Define the holes through which you need to thread the ribbon by pushing through an appropriately sized knitting needle **e**, **f**.

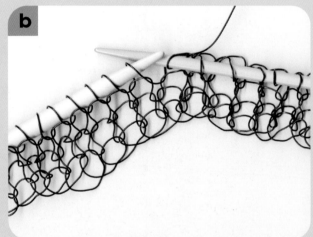

HANDY HINT
Your knitting will 'bunch' up on the needles. Don't worry – you will pull the gauntlet to shape when it is off the needles and complete.

Wire Jewellery

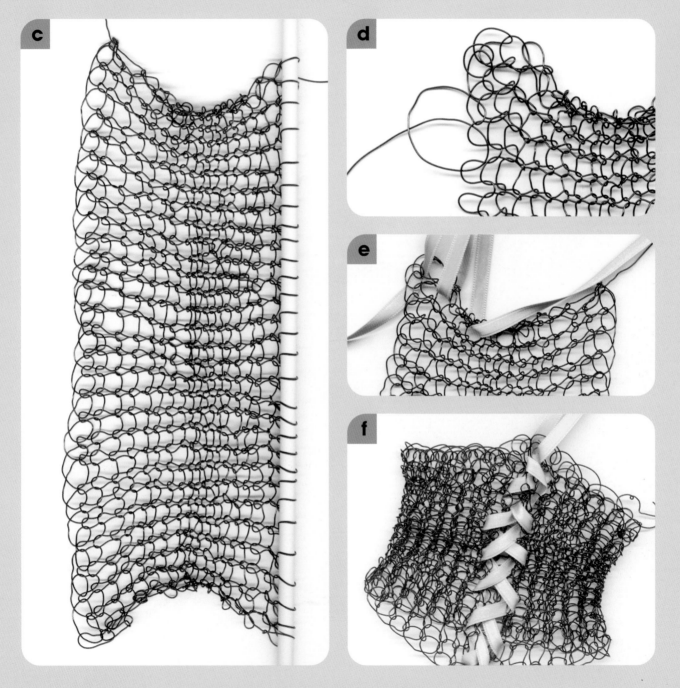

Knitted Gauntlet

VARIATIONS

Below This copper wire cuff has a range of blue beads randomly stitched into the work. It is fastened with a flowing blue ribbon.

Right This cuff is made from solid silver wire and is fastened with a shocking pink ribbon. Rose quartz stones could be incorporated for added effect.

Knitted Gauntlet

Gemstone Crochet Collar

This flattering collar has a lovely delicate appearance. It is made from very thin silver wire and small tumblechip beads. It will fit against the contours of the neck and move with the body. The vibrant carnelian beads shown here are set off perfectly by the silver mesh.

This collar has been designed to showcase the stitches between the rows of stones, and combines double and treble crochets. It would look equally attractive if made with thicker wire, and this will be a necessity if you wish to incorporate heavier beads. Thicker wire will, however, create a more substantial piece of work and, as a result, be less flexible to the touch. Check the tension to determine the required number of stitches.

Equipment
1.5mm (US8 steel) crochet hook
Scissors/wire cutters

Materials
0.2mm (AWG 32, SWG 36) wire, about 82ft (25m)
400 gemstone beads (or the required number)
Fastening

The ends are neatened and supported by rows of double crochet, which also help to strengthen the work where the fastener is to be attached.

It can be made thicker or thinner by varying the number of rows or stitches used, such as all double crochet. A thin collar can look extremely delicate, while thicker ones can be very striking.

The instructions make up a collar that measures approximately 12in (30cm) long. It is advisable, though, to work up a sample before you start using your chosen wire and beads to check the tension and therefore gauge a more accurate length for your individual piece.

HANDY HINT
Make sure that during double crochet rows the beads face away from you, and during treble crochet rows the right side faces you.

Gemstone Crochet Collar

1 Thread the beads onto the wire and make 80 chain stitches plus one turning stitch.

2 Drop a bead into place at the start of the next stitch then double crochet, repeating across the remaining chains **ⓐ**.

3 Make two turning chains, turn the work then treble crochet back along the top of the double crochets in **Row 1 ⓑ**.

4 Make one turning chain then turn the work. Drop a bead into place and double crochet, repeating across the row.

5 Repeat **Steps 3** and **4** twice (giving nine rows in total).

6 To make the edging: without cutting the wire turn the work and double crochet nine stitches along the end of the work (shown in red). Make a turning chain at the start of every row. **ⓒ**

7 Make a further three rows of double crochet, cut the wire. leaving a long end, and pull the end through the last stitch, tightening the knot **ⓓ**.

8 Fold the rows of double crochet under the collar and stitch into place using the end of the wire.

9 At the other end of the collar, repeat the process, making nine double crochet stitches down the end of the collar and stitching the double crochet rows under the work.

10 Gently pull the work into shape and attach the fastening as required **ⓔ**,**ⓕ**.

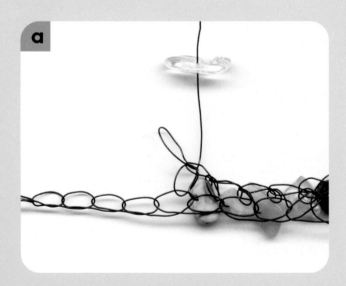

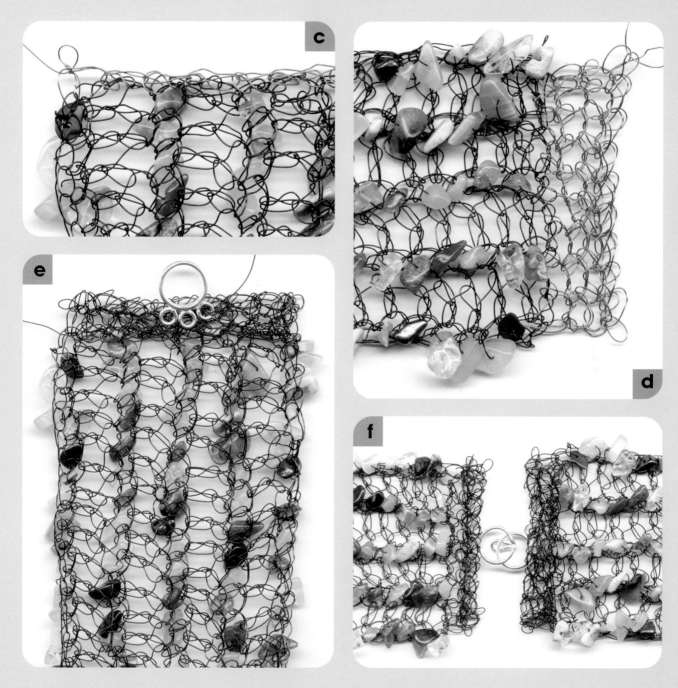

Gemstone Crochet Collar

VARIATIONS

The technique has been adapted in a variety of ways for the neckpieces shown here. They demonstrate how, with just a little imagination, many different items can be created.

Below This collar has been made from rows of double crochet using a tiny crochet hook. Small peridot beads have been incorporated into the bottom row of the collar.

Top right The rock crystal collar is designed to be worn with the fastening at the front. The fastening has been decorated with a beaded crochet wheel (see pages 34–37) and the 'points' have been created from a single row of double crochet.

Bottom right This rose quartz collar is formed using slightly larger beads and a thicker gauge of wire than the other neckpieces.

67

Knitted Flowers

Knitted flowers can be worn in a number of ways. They make unusual brooches if attached to a brooch finding or they can be stitched to a ribbon and worn as a choker. With a pendant finding they make unique and exciting pieces of neckwear, while stitched to a comb they form a pretty headdress.

The three-dimensional rose is made up of individual knitted petals which are pulled into shape and then joined together. The rose illustrated here is formed from six small and four larger petals, but you could make as many as you like.

The thin wispy petals of the daisy tumble outwards to create the effect of a daisy in full bloom. They are made by a series of casting on and casting off which forms the tendrils that are later gathered to become the flower. Silver-plated wire and tiny citrine tumblechip beads have been chosen for this project, as the yellow citrine complements the silver and mimics the colours of a real daisy.

ROSE (shown below left)

Equipment
2mm (US0, UK14) knitting needles
Scissors/wire cutters

Materials
0.2mm (AWG 32, SWG 36) wire, two 82ft (25m)
lengths knitted together

DAISY (shown above left)

Equipment
2mm (US0, UK14) knitting needles
Scissors/wire cutters

Materials
0.2mm (AWG 32, SWG 36) wire, two 56ft (17m)
lengths knitted together
Approximately 18 beads or stones
Findings as required (i.e. brooch or ribbon for choker)

ROSE

The rose is knitted from two strands of 0.2mm wire worked together. Using two strands gives the flower density and firmness while retaining the high degree of flexibility that is found with fine wire and allowing the petals to be knitted on small needles.

The petals are knitted as squares, with shaping across one corner to form the pointed tips. By pulling the work gently diagonally, the square is extended into a shape that resembles a kite. The petals are then cupped in the middle by softly pushing at their centres, and the edges are rolled over and curved to replicate the form of real petals. The wire will hold its shape and can be adjusted further once all the petals have been joined together.

Each petal is given a 'tail' by casting on more stitches than required (see illustration for step 7). When the first row is knitted, the unused cast-on stitches are pulled loose; this forms a chain that is the same as a crocheted chain and can be used to hold the petal and pull it into shape. The creation of the tail will only work if the 'traditional' cast-on method (see page 162) is used; other cast-ons are likely to pull undone, leaving just a kinked bit of wire instead of a chain. The tails can be cut off once you have finished.

The rose can be made larger or smaller by adjusting the number of stitches.

Note: Although the project requires two strands of wire, the step-by-step photographs show the rose made up in single wire so that the process can be clearly seen.

Design Ideas

✻ By assembling the petals in different ways, other flower types can be created – for instance, try arranging the petals to form a poppy.

✻ 'Leaves' can be created by adapting the technique and knitting in a green wire.

✻ By working with two strands of wire, new colour combinations can be explored.

✻ The edges of the roses can be defined further by a row of single crochet.

✻ A rose bud can be made by tightly curling the inner petals then wrapping a couple of larger petals around the inner bud.

Smaller petals

1 Cast on 15 stitches using the technique on page 162 (this is very important or the 'tail' will unravel), knit ten stitches, take the needle from the remaining five cast-on stitches and pull them gently into a chain 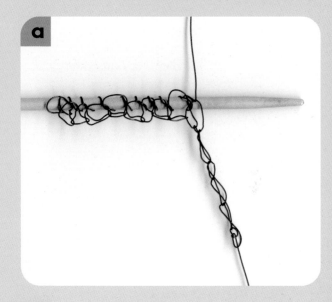.

2 Purl over the next ten stitches and then work another six rows of stocking stitch (one row knit, one row purl, repeated).

3 **Row 9** knit two together, knit to the end of the row (nine stitches).

4 **Row 10** purl to the last two stitches, purl two together (eight stitches).

5 **Row 11** knit two together and knit to the end of the row (seven stitches).

6 **Row 12** purl to the last two stitches, purl two together (six stitches).

7 Cast off the remaining stitches. The petal will look like a square with the corner taken off 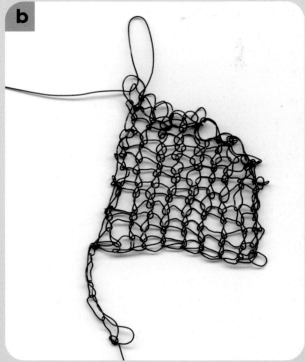. Now shape the petal into a more realistic form by holding the tail with one hand and gently pulling diagonally with the other until you are pleased with the shape.

8 Make another five petals, giving six in total.

Larger petals

9 Using two strands of wire, cast on 17 stitches (again using the technique on page 162 otherwise the 'tail' will unravel), knit 12 stitches, take the needle from the remaining five cast-on stitches and pull them gently into a chain.

10 Purl over the next 12 stitches then work another eight rows of stocking stitch (one row knit, one row purl, repeated).

11 **Row 11** knit two together, knit to the end of the row (11 stitches).

12 **Row 12** purl to the last two stitches, purl two together (ten stitches).

13 **Row 13** knit two together and knit to the end of the row (nine stitches).

14 **Row 14** purl to the last two stitches, purl two together (eight stitches).

15 Cast off the remaining stitches.

HANDY HINT
Joining the petals together takes a steady hand and a large amount of concentration. A willing helper to provide a second pair of hands when doing this will be useful.

Shaping and joining the petals

16 Lay out the petals in front of you. They now need to be pulled into shape. A rose petal is slightly cupped in the middle, curving outwards, and the outer edges gently roll away **c**. The inner petals are slightly rolled to give the appearance of a rose coming out of bud **d**.

17 Pick one of the small petals as the inner petal, curl it into shape and, holding it by its tail, start to build the petals up around it. The tails of the petal will act as an anchor to hold onto. Once the first three or four petals are in position to your liking, wrap some wire around the base to hold them. (This is where the willing friend comes into play.) Wrap the wire around the base a few times and secure it with a twist. This will be covered by the other petals **e**.

18 Continue in this fashion – fixing the petals when you are happy with their position, using the four larger petals round the edge. The tails can be cut off or unpicked as you go, or trimmed at the end if you prefer.

19 Once the rose is complete, wrap some wire firmly and neatly around the base to hold it **f**. The rose can be additionally secured by stitching through the base of the petals.

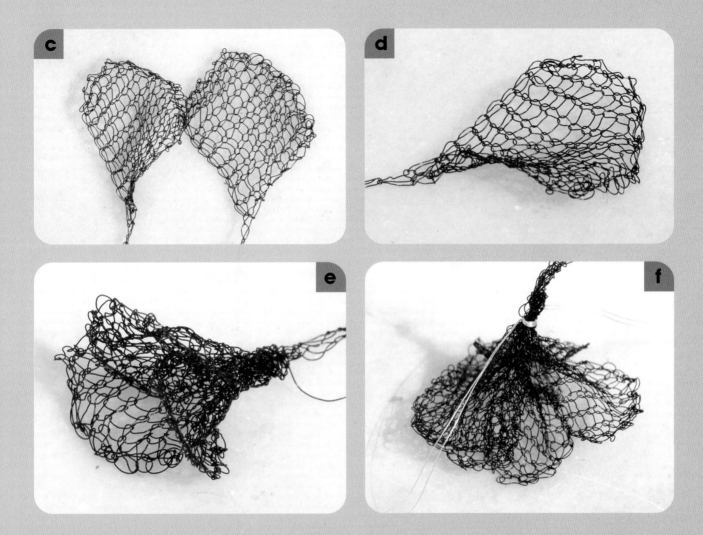

Finishing

20 The rose can be finished as required and would make a very unusual brooch – ideal for a wedding.

DAISY

The daisy is knitted using two strands of very thin wire. This means that the wire is flexible enough to work with thin needles but has more support and density than a single strand, helping it to hold its shape.

HANDY HINTS
This is not a complex project but it is repetitive and therefore can be quite tough on the hands. The constant casting on and casting off with the double wire can be hard on the fingers. A strategically placed sticking plaster can help to prevent any discomfort. Alternatively, knit the daisy over a series of shorter sessions.

This technique is developed further in the Knitted Flower Hair Corsage on pages 96–101 and the Knitted Tendrils Tiara on pages 128–133.

The finished size of the daisy can be altered by adjusting the number of stitches that are cast on and off for each petal or the number of tendrils knitted.

1 Cast on 16 stitches using the traditional method (see page 162) **a**.

2 Cast off 15 stitches, again using the traditional method, leaving one stitch on the needle.

3 Cast on a further 16 stitches (using the stitch from the previous tendril as the foundation stitch for the cast-on but not counting this stitch or working it further).

4 Cast off 15 stitches leaving two stitches on the needle: one from this tendril and one from the previous one **b**.

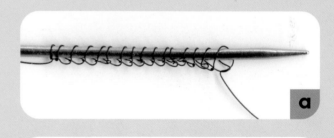

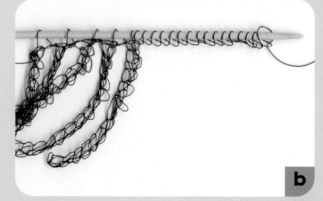

5 Make a further 28 tendrils in the same manner, ensuring that one stitch is left at the base of each tendril, therefore one stitch for each tendril made. When 30 tendrils have been completed there should be 30 stitches left on the needle. Gently pull the tendrils into shape **c** .

6 Knit across the 30 stitches on the needle, ensuring there is a constant tension between each stitch **d** .

7 Repeat this a further three times, giving four rows of knitting in total.

8 Break the wire, gently pull through the stitches **e** then gather the tendrils round to form a circle **f** .

9 Knot the wire and stitch into place.

10 Shape the tendrils into a daisy shape, bending them as required.

11 Stitch the beads into the centre of the daisy by threading a bead onto the wire each time it comes through to the front of the work and then stitching it in place **g** .

12 Finish the daisy as required, such as fixing to a brooch finding or hair comb.

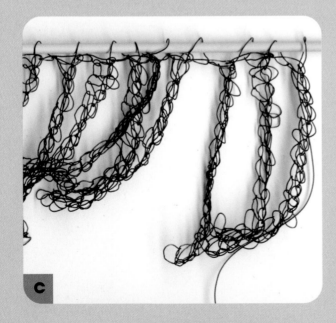

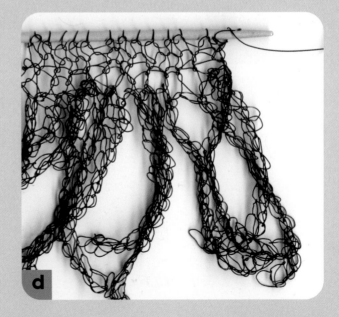

Gemstone Crochet Cuff

This cuff is a beautiful, glittering, golden mass of stones, tightly crocheted using a 1mm (US 11 steel) crochet hook to create a dense mesh. The rich golden citrine beads are set off perfectly by the cool, silver wire.

In this project gemstone beads are crocheted along the entire length of every other row. Irregular-shaped citrine tumblechip beads have been chosen for a natural effect, but regular-sized or calibrated beads could be used to give it a more uniform feel.

HANDY HINT
Citrine is a golden-coloured quartz that varies in colour from light golden to a deep, rich brown. It can be replaced by any other gemstone beads or glass beads.

Equipment
1mm (US11 steel) crochet hook
Scissors/wire cutters

Materials
285 small tumblechip beads (or number required to make the desired size – allow 15 per beaded row)
0.2mm (AWG 32, SWG 36) wire, about 65$\frac{1}{2}$ft (20m)
Bracelet fastening

For this cuff, four rows of plain double crochet are worked before starting to drop the beads into place. This is later folded back and stitched into position under the beginning and at the end of the cuff to give additional stability when attaching the fastener.

Once complete, the mesh can be 'sewn' onto another mesh of the same dimensions, which is made using a thicker wire to provide additional strength. The bracelet can be worn on its own without the supporting mesh, but it won't be as strong.

Gemstone Crochet Cuff

HANDY HINT

When working with a large number of tumblechip beads it is best to thread them onto the wire in batches, as this makes them easier to work with. If this is the first time you have worked with such large quantities then try threading them in batches of around 100 before breaking and rejoining the wire as required.

The finished length of the cuff is approximately 6in (15cm); however, check your tension as you work and adjust the number of rows to ensure you reach your desired length.

Note: The Beaded Knitted Cuff on pages 50–53 is a similar design to this, so for suggestions on how to vary the design see Beaded Knitted Cuff, Variations, pages 54–55.

1 Thread the beads onto the wire.

2 Make a slip knot then make 15 chain stitch. Make one turning chain then turn the work.

3 **Rows 1** to **4** double crochet, making a turning chain before the start of every subsequent new row **a**.

4 **Row 5** drop a stone into place before each stitch, crocheting 15 beads along the length of the row **b**.

5 **Row 6** double crochet.

6 Repeat **Steps 4** and **5** 18 times, or until the cuff reaches the desired length.

7 Next three rows double crochet **c**.

8 Cut the wire, leaving a long end, and draw through the loop, pulling tight.

9 Fold the double crocheted rows at either end under the beaded mesh.

10 Stitch the wire end around the edges of the folded mesh at one end and then repeat at the other end with a new piece of wire.

11 Make an undercuff, if required, to the same dimensions using a thicker grade of wire (shown in red). Stitch into place **d**.

12 Stitch the bracelet fastening into place and tidy up any loose ends **e**.

Gemstone Crochet Cuff

Knitted Chokers

The thin wire used in these projects provides a flexible feel to the finished items, making them comfortable to wear against the neck.

The Classic Choker is simple yet effective. It can either be worn plain to emphasize the complex pattern of the stitches or adorned, perhaps with one of the knitted flowers shown on pages 68–77 or with a beaded wheel (see pages 34–37).

It is knitted and folded in double-thickness silver wire to provide additional strength for embellishments, and the silver lends itself to being combined with a variety of colours and materials.

The Beaded Choker is highly versatile – it can provide the perfect finishing touch to a formal evening dress or be worn with jeans and a casual top to give a glamorous edge to the outfit.

The Rose Quartz Choker is made from a central necklet base, which is sheathed in a rose quartz and silver mesh. The choice of necklet is highly personal. The rubber necklet shown here is a contemporary take on a traditional collar. The deep black of the rubber accentuates the stones and silver. Other ideas include threading a piece of sheer ribbon through the sheath for a truly stunning effect.

CLASSIC (below)

Equipment
2mm (US0, UK14) knitting needles
Scissors/wire cutters

Materials
0.2mm (AWG 32, SWG 36) wire, about 85ft (26m)
Necklace fastener

BEADED (left)

Equipment
2mm (US0, UK14) knitting needles
Scissors/wire cutters

Materials
250 beads (50 beads per beaded row) ranging in
size from $3/16$–$1/4$in (5–6mm)
0.31mm (AWG 29, SWG 30) wire, about 49ft (15m)
Necklace fastener

ROSE QUARTZ (right)

Equipment
2mm (US0, UK14) knitting needles
Scissors/wire cutters

Materials
0.31mm (AWG 29, SWG 30) wire, about 49ft (15m)
450 tumblechip beads (rose quartz)
Necklet

CLASSIC

This choker is knitted in stocking stitch, which consists of alternate rows of knit stitch and purl stitch to give a smooth surface; more texture can be created using garter stitch (every row knit stitch).

The very fine wire and the use of small needles provide a light, open appearance to the meshwork. It is knitted to twice the desired length then doubled over lengthways and stitched together. The collar could be joined by a row of crochet to add additional interest.

The width of the choker is ten stitches, but a narrower collar could also be made with fewer stitches.

1 Cast on ten stitches (or the number of stitches required to create your desired width).

2 Knit in stocking stitch (one row knit, one row purl, repeated) until the choker reaches the desired length when folded double **a**.

3 Fold the choker in half lengthways and gently pull it into shape **b**.

4 Neatly stitch along the edges of the choker (shown in silver) **c**.

5 Attach the fastening **d**.

6 Attach an adornment if you wish, such as the square crocheted in silver and gold wire (left).

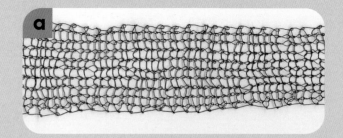

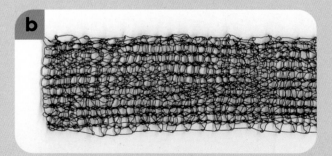

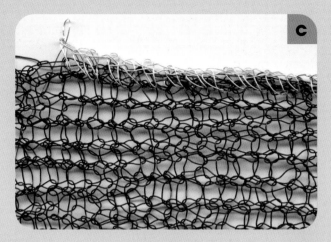

VARIATION

The collar below has been knitted in simple black craft wire and decorated with the 'corsage' shown on pages 96–101.

Other decorations can be attached to this collar, either by stitching or using a jump ring.

The length of the choker can be altered either by reducing or increasing the numbers of stitches or by adjusting the length of the edge pieces. The finished size will also be affected by the size of beads: larger beads will create a larger choker while smaller beads will have the opposite effect. To achieve a certain size, it is best to work a sample piece first to determine the number of stitches required.

BEADED

The Beaded Choker is knitted from top to bottom in stocking stitch (alternate rows of knit stitch and purl stitch). Beads are incorporated into every other row to provide a highly decorative finish. The beads and the black craft wire combine to give an effect that is reminiscent of stained glass.

The beads are dropped into the knitted rows and therefore fall away from you as you work. Stitches are picked up (see page 168) at either side of the collar to knit a mesh, which is then folded and used to attach the fastener.

The picture above shows the choker closed using a vintage clasp that has been renovated with beads to match the choker.

1 Thread your beads onto the wire.

2 Cast on 52 stitches, using the traditional cast-on technique (see page 162).

3 Knit one stitch without beads then knit 50, dropping a bead into place before each stitch and knitting the final stitch without a bead **ⓐ**.

4 Purl one row.

5 Repeat **Steps 3** and **4** a further six times, giving eight rows of beads or the required number **ⓑ**.

6 Knit the last row, dropping a bead into place before each stitch and knitting the first and final stitch without a bead.

7 Cast-off using the traditional technique, but don't break the wire – leave the last loop on the needle **ⓒ**.

8 With the beaded side away from you, pick up the stitches down one edge of the work (see page 168), picking up one stitch per row.

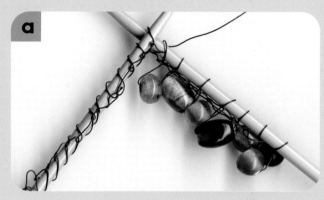

9 Turn the work and, with the beaded side towards you, starting with knit, make eight rows of stocking stitch.

10 Cast off then fold the edges over and stitch into place.

11 Repeat **Steps 8** to **10** on the other side of the collar (this time using a new end of wire).

12 Attach the fastening .

ROSE QUARTZ

This choker has been knitted using a medium-gauge wire (0.31mm/AWG 29, SWG 30), as the sheath needs to retain its shape while holding the weight of the beads but without being stiff. If a thinner wire was used it would probably drag under the weight of the stones and pull the necklet out of shape. It is knitted in a flat piece then stitched together to form a tube.

The finished length of the sheath measures approximately 9½in (24cm). However, this will vary depending on the type of stones used and the tension. Different lengths can be achieved by adjusting the number of stitches. Work up a sample first to determine how many stitches you need to reach your required length.

HANDY HINT
The stitching of the sheath requires a high level of attention to ensure that the sides are equally matched and the stitches are hidden.

1 Pre-bead the wire and cast on 50 stitches using the traditional method (see page 162). Mark every fifth stitch with a twist of wire. (This will help when matching the stitches up at the end as you stitch the piece together.)

2 Dropping a bead into place before each stitch, knit one row.

3 Purl the next row.

4 Dropping a bead into place before each stitch, knit the next row **ⓐ** .

5 Repeat **Steps 3** and **4** three times, making nine rows knitted in total, ending on a knit row.

6 Cast off, leaving a long tail to stitch the sheath up with. Mark each fifth stitch with a twist of wire as it is cast off **ⓑ** .

7 Stitch the sheath up the side using the cast-off tail then tie off the end. It is important that this stitching is accurate so as to provide a smooth appearance to the work. The stitch markers in the cast-on and cast-off rows can be matched to ensure the sheath is neatly stitched **ⓒ** .

8 Thread the necklet through the sheath **ⓓ** .

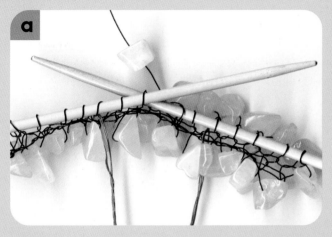

VARIATION

Using the same technique a longer sheath can be made and threaded onto ribbon. It is worn with the opening to the front and the ribbon tied in a bow.

Crochet Tendrils Collar

This collar features a mass of tendrils that fall around the neck. The tendrils graduate in length, reaching a 'V' at the front. This is a fantastic neckpiece, which looks equally stunning made either in craft wire with a selection of glass beads (shown here) or with silver wire and gemstones, shown on page 95.

Fine silver wire has been used to make this collar, giving it an extremely light, almost textile feel. Consequently, it moves with the body rather than hanging stiffly. To support the lightweight structure an 'undercollar' of medium-weight wire has been made for the tendrils to fit to. It helps to prevent the neckpiece from pulling out of shape, but it is an optional feature.

HANDY HINT
Because this collar uses a large number of beads the wire will need to be threaded in batches. As one batch of beads is used the wire should be cut and restrung. Follow the technique on page 167 for joining wire.

Materials
0.2mm (AWG 32, SWG 36) wire, about 65½ft (20m)
Approximately 620 beads
0.31mm (AWG 29, SWG 30) wire, about 23ft (7m)
Fastening

Equipment
2mm (USB-0, UK14) crochet hook
Scissors/wire cutters
Notepad and pen for keeping account of progress

Crochet Tendrils Collar

A tendril is formed over two rows, with the first row being non-beaded and the second row beaded. The tendril foundation chain is made at the end of every non-beaded row and the beads are worked in on the return in the beaded row. The shaping at the front is made over 15 tendrils by increasing or decreasing the number of foundation chain. (The illustrations opposite show these steps.)

HANDY HINTS
Make sure you keep count as the collar progresses so as not to lose your place.

The main body of the collar is made over 12 stitches; this does not alter throughout. The tendril is measured from the end of the main body.

The size of the collar can be adjusted either by reducing or increasing the number of rows. The type of clasp that fastens the collar can also provide a degree of flexibility as to the end fit.

Remember to make a turning stitch at the start of each row and do not crochet into the turning stitch.

1 Thread the first batch of beads onto the wire.

Note: This project uses a lot of beads so string as many as you are comfortable handling in one sitting.

2 Make a foundation chain of 12.

3 Work six rows of double crochet.

4 **First tendril** double crochet across the 12 stitches which form the main body and, at the end of the row, make four chain plus a turning chain **ⓐ** .

5 Dropping a bead into place before each double crochet, miss the turning stitch and return double crocheting along the four stitches of the tendril foundation chain and along the 12 stitches that form the main body of the collar (16 stitches in total). Remember that a tendril is formed of only two rows **ⓑ** .

6 Repeat **Steps** **4** and **5** seven times  to give eight tendrils in total. Place a marker at the end of this tendril to mark the start of the shaping.

7 The next 15 tendrils form the shaped part of the collar, the first seven tendrils are increased, then the eighth is the central tendril and the last seven are the decreased section. To make the increased tendrils repeat **Steps** **4** and **5** above seven times but increase the tendril chain by two each time so that the seventh shaped tendril is 18 stitches long (not including the turning chain) plus the 12 stitches of the main body of the collar.

8 The eighth shaped tendril is the central one. Make the tendril 22 stitches long (plus 12 stitches of the main body of the collar) .

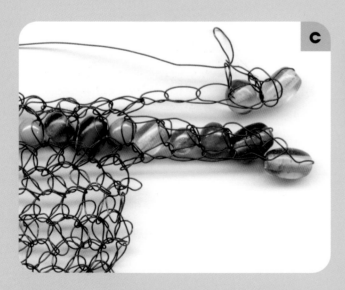

Crochet Tendrils Collar

9 To form the decreased tendrils, reverse the instructions in **Step 8**, with the first tendril being 18 stitches long and then each subsequent tendril decreased by two until the seventh tendril is six stitches long.

10 Repeat **Steps 5** and **6** above eight times to complete the end of the tendrils.

11 Double crochet six rows.

12 Gently pull each tendril into shape.

Undercollar

13 The undercollar provides support to the light, lacy mesh of the tendril collar. It is crocheted from 0.3mm (AWG 29, SWG 30) wire, the length of the collar, then stitched into place **e**.

14 Attach a finding as required **f**.

VARIATIONS

The technique of making tendrils can be adapted by using different stones or beads or by varying the length of the tendrils. A lot of beads are used in the creation of the collar, so it is best not to use overly large beads, otherwise it may prove too heavy to wear.

Top right This dramatic collar been made using garnet stones.

Centre right This dramatic 'Ice Queen' collar uses a mass of rock crystal beads.

Bottom right An entirely different effect is created by using tendrils of the same length.

Below The orange earrings have been made using the same technique but with just three tendrils. The length of the tendrils can easily be adjusted and you can choose stones to match a collar.

Crochet Tendrils Collar

Knitted Flower Hair Corsage

This beautiful knitted headdress comprises three pieces that are stitched together at the end to form the finished piece. The flower has tendrils winding around it from one side, with longer tendrils providing additional curls.

The flower is knitted on two different-sized needles using two strands of wire for extra strength. It is then gathered together once complete. The tendrils are made by casting on a row and then casting off immediately. They, too, are gathered and shaped around the central flower. The tendrils hold their form well and can be bent or curled into place around a pencil or pen.

The inner part of the flower is formed using the tendril technique of casting on and off and combines pearl and crystal beads for added interest. It could be knitted in a different colour for contrast.

Equipment

2mm (US0, UK14) knitting needles
6mm (US10, UK4) knitting needles
Small crochet hook
Scissors/wire cutters

Materials

Two strands of 0.2mm (AWG 32, SWG 36) wire, each about 82ft (25m)
16 beads (8 x pearls, 8 x 3⁄16in (5mm) Bicone crystal beads)
Hair comb

Design Ideas

- The finished flower has been fastened to a comb to wear as a headdress, but it would look equally stunning if worn as a brooch or perhaps fastened to a length of ribbon to form a choker (see page 85 for an example of this).
- Vary the tightness of the tendrils' curls by winding them around a small knitting needle for tighter curls or a thicker needle for looser curls.
- A lightweight structure can be created by using a single strand of wire.
- Alternative effects can be achieved by using different-coloured wires and perhaps also using two colours together.
- The length and number of tendrils can be varied to change the look and feel of the piece; for instance. adding longer tendrils will give a larger and more extravagant finished effect. Beads can also be incorporated at the end of the tendrils to add sparkle or colour to the design.

Knitted Flower Hair Corsage

The main flower is created by casting on with the larger-size needles then working three rows of stocking stitch on a smaller needle. The number of stitches are then reduced over two rows and the remaining stitches gathered together to form a 'rosette'-style flower.

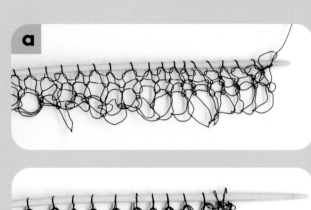

Main flower

1 Using two strands of wire together, cast on 100 stitches with the larger set of knitting needles.

2 Change to the smaller knitting needles and work three rows of stocking stitch (knit one row, purl one row and knit one row) or three rows of garter stitch (knit every row), as preferred 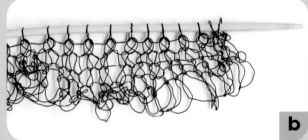.

3 Knit two together and repeat across the entire row (leaving 50 stitches on the needle) **b**.

4 Knit two together and repeat across the remaining stitches (leaving 25 stitches on the needle) **c**.

5 Break the wire and draw the ends through the remaining stitches.

6 Gather the flower together into a rosette style, shaping as required **d**, **e**.

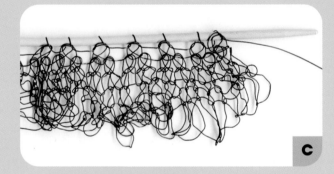

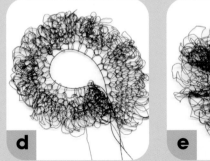

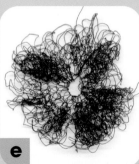

Inner flower

Note: **Each prong has two different-coloured beads on the end. Thread the beads onto the wire alternately. The prongs are graduated in length so they can be shaped in the centre of the flower; however, they can be made the same length if preferred.**

7 Thread the beads onto the two strands of wire that are to be worked.

8 Cast on four stitches, dropping a bead into the last two stitches.

9 Cast off three stitches, leaving one stitch on the needle.

10 Cast on five stitches, dropping a bead into place on the last two stitches. (Do not count the stitch left on the needle from the last 'tendril' or prong.)

11 Cast off four stitches, leaving two stitches on the needle **f**.

12 Repeat the cast-on and cast-off process another six times, increasing one stitch each time and dropping the beads into the last two stitches.

13 Eight stitches will be left on the needle, knit two rows over these eight stitches.

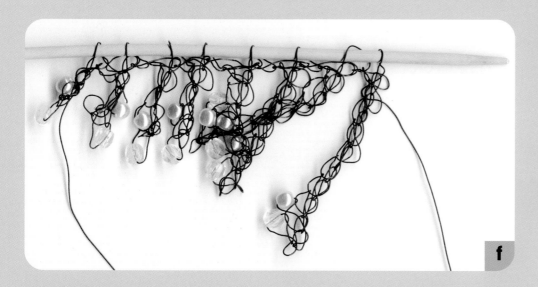

Knitted Flower Hair Corsage

14 Cut off the wire and draw the ends through the remaining stitches on the needle **g**.

15 Wind the work tightly into a circle and pull the prongs into shape **h**.

16 Twist the gathered end together into a point and tuck into the centre of the flower. Stitch into place.

Tendrils

You will create 30 tendrils of varying lengths.

17 Working with two strands of wire together, cast on 26 stitches, using the traditional cast-on.

18 Cast off 25 stitches, leaving one stitch on the knitting needle.

19 Repeat eight times, giving nine tendrils in total with nine stitches remaining on the knitting needle.

20 Repeat the above, casting on and off 30 stitches to create a further nine tendrils.

21 Repeat again, casting on and off 35 stitches to create nine more tendrils and giving 27 stitches on the needle.

22 Make three more tendrils, casting on and off 50 stitches to create the long tendrils. There should now be 30 stitches on the needle.

23 Knit three rows over the 30 stitches on the needle **i**.

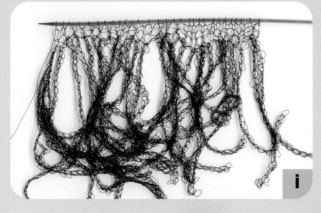

24 Cut off the wire, leaving a long end, and draw the wire through the 30 stitches on the needle. It may be easier to use a small crochet hook to draw the wire through **j**.

25 The tendrils should now be gathered into a shape that complements the flower; the longer tendrils can be shaped or curled by winding around a pen or knitting needle **k**.

Finishing

26 The tendrils and flower should now be stitched together using the ends of the wire. The ends can then be tied off and hidden within the work. As they are stitched together, the tendrils and the flower can be shaped as required **l**.

27 The finished piece should be fastened to a hair comb or a different finding if preferred.

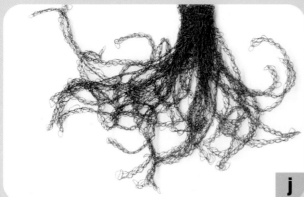

Knitted Flower Hair Corsage

Crochet Chunky Necklace

This necklace is made by crocheting a mass of tumblechip gemstone beads around a core chain. The irregular shape of the beads and the dense stitches create a very tactile piece of jewellery.

The technique involves treble crocheting wire continuously around a core chain. As the stitches progress they naturally form a spiral, which works its way up the chain, completely enclosing it in stitches. This not only gives the jewellery added strength and stability, it also provides a high degree of movement and flexibility. (The illustration for Step 7 on page 105 shows how the spiral is formed).

HANDY HINTS
Any chain can be used for the core, but it is worth ensuring it is reasonably strong. If in doubt, pull the chain between your hands and see if it snaps under gentle pressure. If required, the core chain can be reinforced by some heavy-duty beading wire. Also, while the core chain can be made from any material, it is prudent to match the chain to the wire; for instance, if using solid silver wire choose a silver core chain to ensure the work isn't spoilt by the inner core tarnishing.

The quantities of materials stated are only a guide. Probably more so than any other project, this necklace will be affected by the hook size, tension, type of stones/beads and stitch density.

Equipment
2mm (USB-O, UK14) crochet hook
Scissors/wire cutters

Materials
0.2mm (AWG 32, SWG 36) wire, about 197ft (60m)
900 tumblechip gemstone beads
Two heavy-duty jump rings
Necklace fastener
Core chain of the desired length

This is probably the most time-consuming project in the book – many hours will be spent threading the beads and crocheting them into a rope. However, the finished item is well worth the time. It is best not to scrimp on materials, as, given a bit of care, this necklace will last a lifetime, so it would be a shame to spoil it by using inferior materials.

The stitches in this project are anchored with a jump ring at either end. Choose a strong jump ring, as this is a heavy piece of jewellery. (Make sure, though, that it will fit through a link of the core chain.) You could also give some thought to using a self-locking jump, which will lock the jump ring without the need to solder. This will stop the wires from pulling through or the jump ring coming open.

HANDY HINT
Keep the beads and stitches tight, pushing them up the core chain if necessary.

1 Thread the beads onto the wire.

2 Fasten a jump ring to each end of the core chain **ⓐ**.

3 Make a slip knot in the wire **ⓑ**.

4 This step 'fastens' the crochet around the core chain. Hold the core chain in your left-hand, put the hook through the slip knot and bring it under the core wire, make a chain stitch (this encompasses the core chain) **ⓒ**. Make a further chain stitch.

5 Drop a bead into place **ⓓ** then make a treble crochet stitch as close to the jump ring as possible, using the core chain as a foundation to anchor the stitch **ⓔ**.

6 Repeat dropping a bead into place at the start of each new treble crochet stitch that is worked around the core chain **ⓕ**. The stitches will naturally spiral around the core chain – do not force them or the work will end up uneven **ⓖ**. The number of stitches required to form a complete row around the core chain will very much depend on the tension, bead size, the individual user, and so on. Remember to occasionally untwist the end of chain in the left hand, which will also be twisting in the other direction as the spiral is created.

7 Repeat **Step 6** above until the spiral meets the jump ring at the top. Illustration **ⓗ** shows how the spiral is formed – note that this has been pulled loose to illustrate the process; your work will be a lot tighter.

8 Cut the wire and pull the end through the last loop to secure it. Finish and tidy the piece by threading the end into the work. Gently pull the necklace into shape and fasten a necklace finding as required.

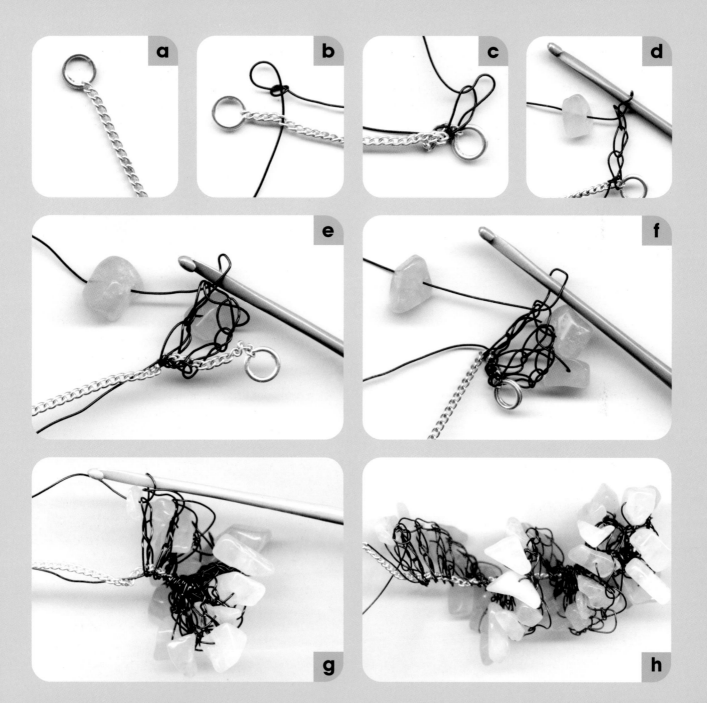

Crochet Chunky Necklace

VARIATIONS

The variations shown here demonstrate how the use of different beads and stones can have a dramatic effect on the finished item. The combination of a variety of glass beads in similar colours and shades produces a beautifully textured and unusual item.

The technique can be adapted further by using alternative wire gauges or different-sized hooks. Try making the necklace without beads or with very tiny beads to highlight the pattern of the stitch detail.

Below A range of coloured glass beads and stones create different effects

Top right Labradite tumblechip stones.

Bottom right The mix of glass beads in this necklace gives a rich and varied texture.

Far right The unusual shape of these carnelian teardrop beads creates a very interesting and highly textured item.

Crochet Chunky Necklace

Knitted Tendrils Neckpiece

This striking neckpiece is designed to hang off a chain or choker. The long, delicate tendrils tumble around the collarbone.

Small tumblechip topaz stones have been knitted into the work. The cool blue topaz complements the silver wire and catches the light beautifully.

An undercollar has been knitted separately and attached to the rear of the neckpiece. It is knitted in a thicker wire, which gives the collar additional strength along the top to support the lightweight structure without restricting or compromising the intricate feel of the piece. The knitted undercollar also provides a band through which a chain or wire can be threaded.

Equipment
2mm (US0, UK14) knitting needles
Scissors/wire cutters

Materials
Approximately 500 beads
0.2mm (AWG 32, SWG 36) wire, about 49ft (15m)
0.4mm (AWG 26, SWG 27) wire (or a gauge thick enough to provide support), about $16\frac{1}{2}$ft (5m)
Chain, choker or wire as required

Design Ideas

✿ The number or length of the tendrils can be altered to give the finished item a different shape. Here with each row the tendrils have been gradually increased, but a more dramatic effect could be achieved by making radical increases or by randomly varying the length.

✿ Use different stones, beads or coloured wire to create a variety of effects.

✿ If a more substantial piece of jewellery is required, the wire can be substituted for a thicker gauge, or two strands of wire can be worked together.

This neckpiece is knitted from side to side in stocking stitch (one row knit stitch, one row purl repeated) with small needles to create a tight mesh. The beads are knitted into every knit row, which makes the beaded side the right side. The main body of the neckpiece is made over 15 stitches.

The tendrils are knitted by casting on a number of stitches then casting off the next row, using the traditional method of both. Beads are incorporated within the cast-off process of each tendril.

Neckpiece

1 Cast on 27 stitches.

2 Cast off the first 12 stitches, dropping a bead into position between each stitch of the cast-off **a**.

3 Knit the remaining 15 stitches, dropping a bead into place between each stitch **b**.

4 Purl across the 15 stitches on the needle **c**.

5 Turn the work and cast on 14 stitches **d**.

6 Cast off the 14 stitches, beading as before, and knit over the remaining 15 stitches, dropping a bead into place **e**.

7 Repeat the process **f**, increasing the number of tendril stitches cast on each time by two to 30, then decreasing by two back to 12. On the last row, cast off the entire piece. Remember that the beaded row is the cast-off/knitted row.

Undercollar

8 Cast on six stitches using the thicker gauge of wire then continue in stocking stitch until the undercollar measures the same length as the finished neckpiece.

9 Securely stitch the neckpiece into place along the top and the bottom of the undercollar, leaving either end open to allow for a chain, or similar, to be threaded through.

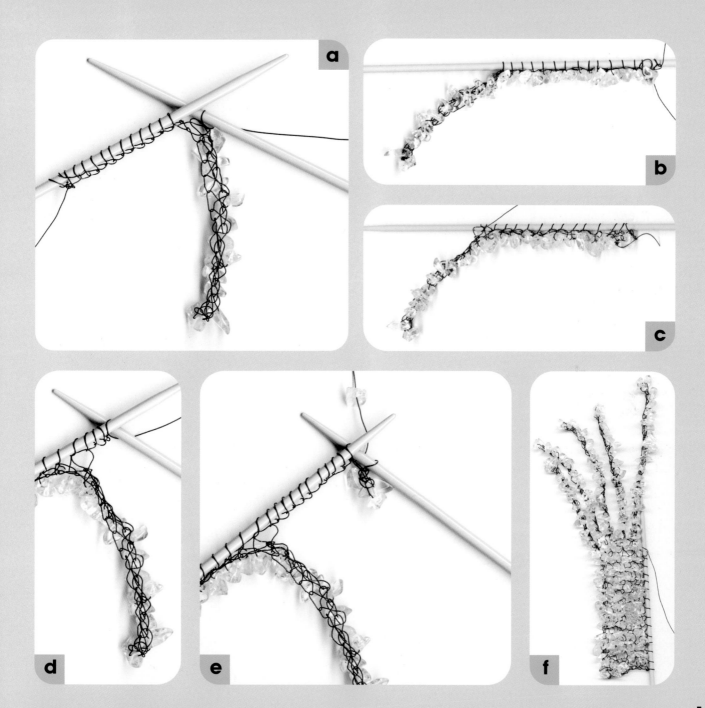

Knitted Tendrils Neckpiece

Knitted Crowns

These unusual knitted crowns are really striking. They will provide the perfect accessory to any wedding or special-occasion outfit.

The Fairytale Crown is knitted in a shocking pink craft wire for a very unusual effect; however, made in silver-plated wire a much more traditional look could be achieved. It is designed to sit on top of the head and is made in such a way that it doesn't need to be fastened to a tiara or crown base but can be held in place with hairgrips or slides. A single row of beads gives detail to the crown band.

Knitted in a medium-weight wire, it is light and airy but robust enough to hold its shape. The points are assembled so that they overlap, which gives the finished structure its strength.

Instructions have been given for knitting this crown in a flat piece using two needles and then stitching it together, but experienced knitters may prefer to make this 'in the round' using circular or four needles.

The Princess Crown is ideal for a bride looking for an unusual but discreet headdress, or for a junior bridesmaid or party princess.

HANDY HINT
Although the wire and the needle size can be substituted, these crowns are best knitted on small needles to ensure a tight mesh that will support its own weight.

FAIRYTALE (right)

Equipment
Long 2mm (US0, UK14) knitting needles
Scissors/wire cutters

Materials
0.3mm (AWG 29, SWG 36) wire, about 164ft (50m)
50 beads

PRINCESS (page 118)

Equipment
Long 2mm (US0, UK14) knitting needles
Scissors/wire cutters

Materials
0.5mm (AWG 24, SWG 25) wire, about 46ft (14m)
8 lightweight beads – six $\frac{1}{4}$in (6mm) beads and two $\frac{5}{16}$in (8mm) beads. (The beads need to be lightweight so as not to pull the finished points over; acrylic hollow beads are ideal.)

Knitted Crowns

FAIRYTALE

This crown is made up of individual points that are joined together at the end. The points are knitted starting at the tip and then increased gradually to form a triangle. Knitting a sample point will allow the finished size to be determined and any adjustments made.

The points are carefully removed from the needle with the stitches intact (note that the stitches will not run or come undone). Then, when each one is complete, they are assembled onto a needle and knitted into the crown base. Each point is joined to the middle of the next point; therefore, in effect, the crown has two rows of points, one behind the other. To measure the base of the crown one row of points needs to be counted; in this instance, ten points, giving a measurement of about 9in (22.5cm) from side to side or circumference of 17in (44cm).

The base of the crown is knitted to a length and then doubled over, giving it the support required to not need a crown or tiara base; however, if preferred, one can be used to give added strength.

HANDY HINT
The fairytale crown works with a large number of stitches when the points are joined and a long pair of knitting needles will be useful (18in/45cm or longer). If these are not available then using a circular needle will ensure that all the stitches are held on the needle (using the circular needle like ordinary knitting needles and knitting from left to right unless knitting in the round).

The size of the crown can be adjusted by varying the number of points; however, because of the overlapping construction of the crown there needs to be an equal number of points.

To make the points

The points are formed by increasing the work in each row, starting with a single stitch. The increases are made by wrapping the wire over the needle to form an additional loop. This is done between the penultimate and the final stitch on each row, ensuring that the work is increased progressively and consistently.

1 Make a slip knot.

2 Knit into the stitch then move the stitch back onto the left-hand needle.

3 Cast on a second stitch and knit both stitches.

4 Knit one, take the wire over your needle to create a new stitch, knit one giving three stitches on the needle.

5 Each and every subsequent row: knit into each stitch, making a stitch between the last and penultimate stitch (make each stitch by wrapping the wire over the needle).

6 Continue in this manner until there are 20 stitches on the needle 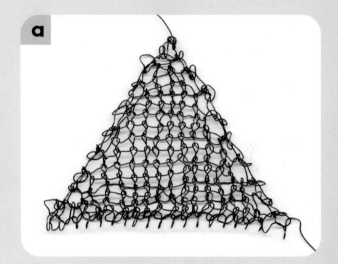.

7 Cut the wire and carefully remove the triangle (do not cast off). The work will not come undone and can be placed carefully to one side until all the points are completed; however, if a spare needle is available the finished points can be slipped onto it for safekeeping.

8 Make another nine points, giving ten in total (or the required number). When all the points have been made they need to be joined so that each one overlaps the next. The stitches of each point therefore need to sit alternately on the needle and this is best done laying the points out as in illustration 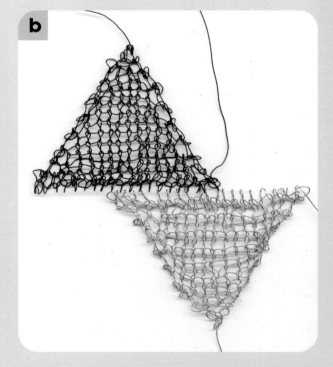. The aim is to get the stitches as evenly placed over the needle as possible and the stitches from each point to alternate across the needle. However, if the odd stitch slips out of sequence it is really not going to make any difference to the finished item. Do ensure that all the points are facing the same way on the needle – the cut end of wire should be facing the pointed end of the needle.

Knitted Crowns

Joining the points and making the crown band

9 Thread the stitches of the points onto the needle, giving 200 stitches in total **c**, **d**.

10 Cast off the first ten stitches of the first point that don't overlap the neighbouring point.

11 Starting with the first two stitches (a stitch from each point) knit two stitches together across the entire row **e**.

12 If using beads, knit a bead into every alternate stitch.

13 Knit a further nine rows, giving ten rows of the band in total **f**.

14 Cast off – as the band is going to be turned over and stitched into place, there is no need to cast off using the traditional method; instead, thread a piece of wire through the stitches to hold them in place.

15 Using the ends of the wire, stitch the points together where they join.

16 Join the two ends of the crown, overlapping the points, and stitch into place **g**.

17 Turn the band under itself and stitch into place, stitching in the final row of stitches.

18 Neaten and tidy any loose ends of wire. The wire at the tip of each point can be tidied by bending it into a loop and wrapping the end of wire neatly around the base.

19 If using a tiara or crown base, the finished crown can be stitched to the base. The size of the crown may need to be adjusted to fit.

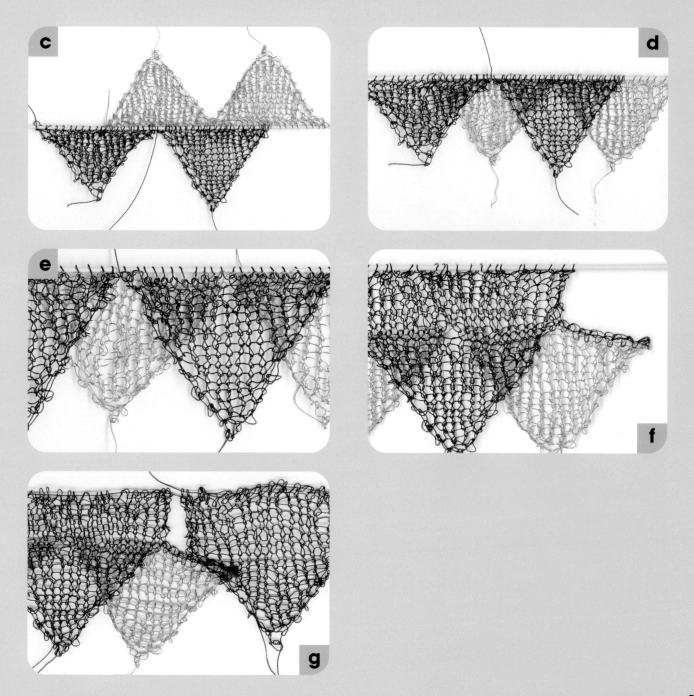

PRINCESS

The Princess Crown is made up of individual pieces that are assembled at the end and knitted onto a knitted shallow crown band. It is created using thick wire and small needles, which gives it strength and ensures it holds its form without the points needing to overlap.

Each point is topped with a lightweight bead. (It is important that the beads are not too heavy, as they may otherwise pull the points down.)

The finished crown is robust enough to not require a purchased crown or tiara base – it has been designed to be secured with hairgrips – but one can be added if you prefer.

The dimensions of the crown are small enough to fit a young person. However, it is very straightforward to increase the size by simply adding further points.

HANDY HINT
The combination of thick wire and small needles may prove difficult to work with. If so, an equally strong structure can be made with multiple strands of a thinner wire.

To make the points

The points are formed by increasing the work in each row, starting with a single stitch. The increases are made by wrapping the wire over the needle to create an additional loop. This is done between the penultimate and final stitch on each row, ensuring the work is increased progressively and consistently.

1 Make a slip knot.

2 Knit into the stitch then move the stitch back onto the left-hand needle.

3 Cast on a second stitch and knit both stitches.

4 Knit one, take your wire over the needle to create a new stitch, knit one, giving three stitches on the needle.

5 Each and every subsequent row: knit into each stitch, making a stitch between the last and penultimate stitch (make a stitch by wrapping the wire over the needle).

6 Continue in this manner until there are ten stitches on the needle. The point might need pulling into shape **ⓐ**.

7 Cut the wire and carefully remove the triangle (do not cast off). The work will not come undone and can be placed carefully to one side until all the points are complete (however, if a spare needle is available the finished points can be slipped onto it for safekeeping).

8 Make another seven points.

9 Each of the eight points must now be carefully replaced onto the needle. It is important to ensure that each point is facing in the right direction. The cut end of the wire should be towards the tip of the needle. There will be 80 stitches on the needle **ⓑ**.

10 Knit across the 80 stitches, paying particular attention to keeping the tension tight where two points join. Repeat five times, giving six rows of garter stitch **ⓒ**.

11 Remove the work from the needles, cut the wire and thread a piece of wire through the stitches to secure them. There is no need to cast off with a traditional method, as the work will be held when it is stitched in place. Fold the crown base back upon itself and stitch into place **ⓓ**. Join the two ends together, making the crown into a circle, and gently pull the points into shape.

12 Tidy and fasten off the loose wire between the points. An additional 'stitch' can be made between the points for extra strength if required.

13 Attach a bead to the tip of each point using the end of the wire from the cast-on. Slide the bead down the wire to the point then fix in place, making a small loop and winding the wire neatly around itself **ⓔ**.

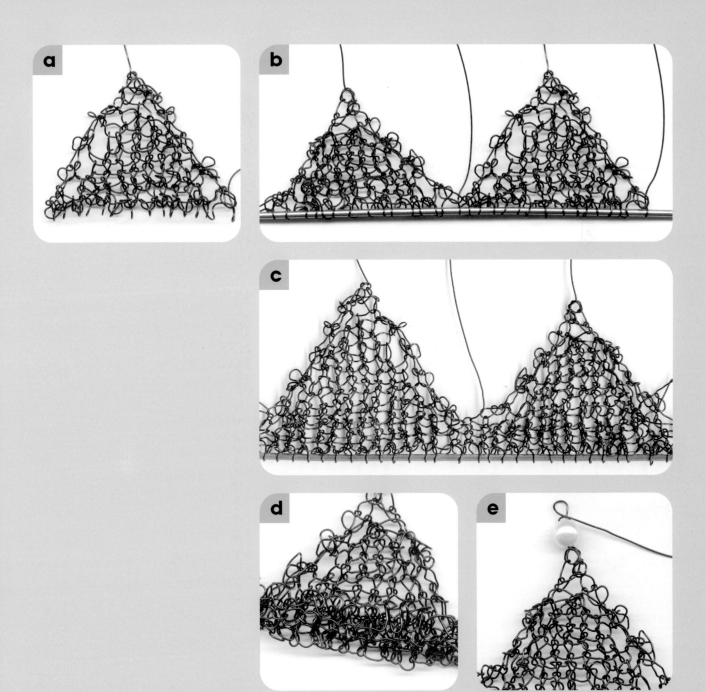

Crochet Tiara

This tiara combines crocheted wire with high-quality Czech crystal beads, giving a sparkle to the finished piece and accentuating the detail of the stitches. It is a beautiful accessory and perfect for a bride.

The tiara is created using double strands of thin wire and a very small crochet hook. This gives it enough strength to hold its shape while still allowing tight stitches to be made. Here it has been crocheted in purple and black wire to give the effect of a deep midnight plum colour. Two different-coloured beads have been used to complement the two colours of the wire. For a more traditional look, however, silver wires with pearls and clear crystal would work very well.

Equipment
1mm (US11 steel) crochet hook
Scissors/wire cutters

Materials
Two strands of 0.2mm (AWG 32, SWG 36) wire, each about 131ft (40m)
94 crystal beads (39 purple and 55 black), approximately $5/32$in (4mm) in size

HANDY HINT
If you decide to vary or adapt the design, remember that the tiara needs to have sufficient strength to hold its shape and not bend under its own weight. A taller design, or one using more or heavier beads, will need to be crocheted in thicker wires.

Design Idea

✄ Paint your tiara band using a complementary shade of nail varnish to help it blend with the finished work.

Crochet Tiara

Tiara band

This design combines different crochet stitches and uses treble clusters. Treble clusters are made by crocheting a number of trebles into a single stitch so that they form a semicircle. The beaded loops at the top of the tiara are made using a beaded chain, which is then joined into a loop. The tiara is graduated in height by building up the rows on the central stitches. It is created in one flat piece then attached to a tiara band once complete.

HANDY HINT
The wires need to be broken before the beaded rows and re-strung at that point; this is to avoid having to pull the wires through the beads in non-beaded rows, which might damage the coated surface. While this means more wires to tidy up at the end, it ensures the coating has not been worn away to leave exposed copper (obviously not an issue if coated wires are not being used i.e. solid silver). Before you start, decide on the required pattern of the beads. In the illustrated tiara the beads have been placed so that they fall alternately. If you wish to use a different combination then the beads will need to be strung accordingly.

The tiara measures approximately 13¾in (35cm) in length and 2in (5.5cm) at the tallest point. However, the size can easily be adjusted or made to fit a crown fitting rather than a tiara band if required.

1 Make a chain of 101 stitches, make a turning chain and turn the work.

2 Double crochet four rows over these 101 stitches, making a turning chain at the end of each row (do not crochet into the turning chain) **ⓐ**.

3 Thread 51 beads (26 purple, 25 black, if you wish to replicate the tiara shown on page 123, alternating the colours and starting with a purple bead) onto two strands of wire.

4 **Beaded row** the first stitch is a plain double crochet and is followed by three beaded double crochet and three plain double crochet. This is repeated along the row, ending with a single plain double crochet. The middle bead stitch forms the centre of the next row of treble clusters. The beads will fall to the rear of the work, making this the right side **ⓑ**.

5 **First row of treble clusters** do not make a turning chain. Missing the first two stitches, make five trebles into the next stitch (i.e. the central beaded stitch from the previous row). Miss the next two stitches and then double crochet into the next stitch (which is the central stitch of the three non-beaded stitches of the previous row). Repeat to the end of the row. Cut the wire then fasten and tidy the end **ⓒ**.

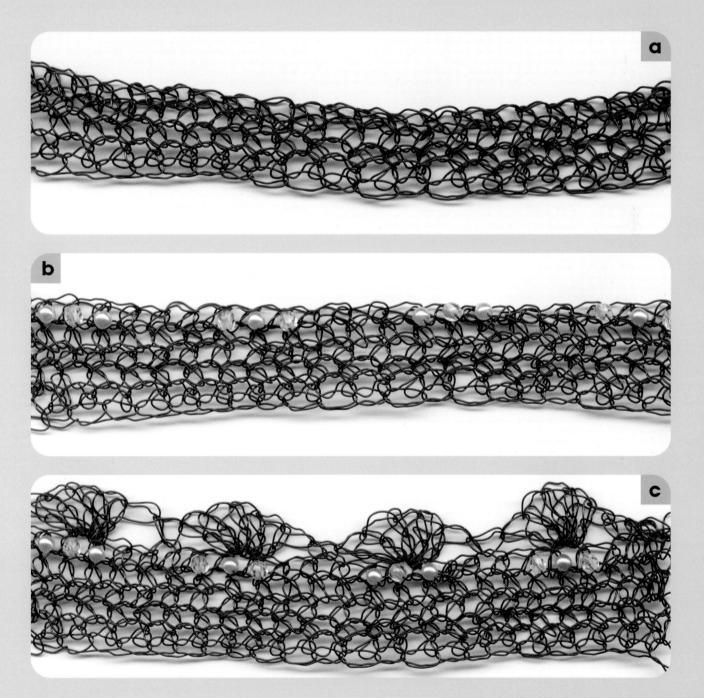

6 **Chain row** thread 13 beads onto the two strands of wire (seven purple, six black, alternating the colour and starting with a purple bead). With the beaded side to the rear of the work, miss the first two clusters, and into the middle stitch of the third cluster make one double crochet, dropping the first bead into place. Make five chain and double crochet into the middle stitch of the next cluster, dropping a bead into place. Repeat so that 13 clusters in total have a beaded double crochet worked into the central stitch (i.e. the two clusters at either end have not been worked) **d**.

7 **Second row of treble clusters** turn the work, make two chain and then double crochet into the third stitch of the chain of the previous row. Make five treble stitches into the beaded stitch of the previous row to form one treble cluster, double crochet into the middle chain and then make a treble cluster into the next beaded stitch. Repeat to the penultimate beaded stitch, treble cluster into this stitch, double crochet into the middle stitch of the chain then make two chain, fastening this with a single crochet in the last beaded stitch. Break the wire and fasten neatly **e**.

8 **Finishing row** the final row makes the detail across the top of the tiara. The beaded 'points' or loops have been made by crocheting the beaded chain into a loop. A single bead is dropped into place at either side of these points. Note the step-by-step photographs show the item made up with pearl beads. If you wish to replicate the tiara shown at the start of the project the beads need to be strung as follows: 1 purple, 3 black, 1 purple, 5 black, 1 purple, 7 black, 1 purple, 5 black, 1 purple, 3 black, 1 purple.

9 Starting in the middle cluster of the previous row, make one double crochet, dropping a bead into place. Make five chain and single crochet into the middle of the next cluster. Make three chain, dropping a bead into each chain stitch, and single crochet into the same stitch to give a small loop. Make five chain and then double crochet into the centre of the next cluster, dropping a bead into place. Repeat to the end of the row, with the next loop being five beaded chain, the middle one being seven beaded chain and the remaining two being five and three respectively. End with a single beaded double crochet in the last cluster **f**.

10 Fasten off and tidy loose ends. Gently pull the work into shape.

11 Stitch to a tiara band as required.

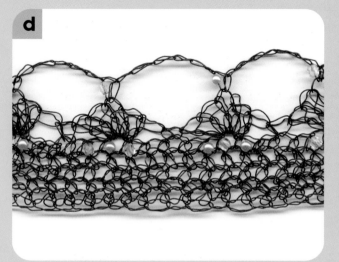

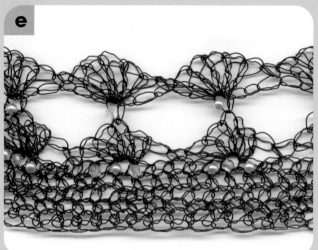

Crochet Tiara

Knitted Tendrils Tiara

This is a very unusual headdress, with a mass of silver tendrils curling organically around each other. The inclusion of Swarovski crystals and glass pearls add sparkle and interest, catching the light as you move.

One of the key features of the design is the way the tendrils are massed together, providing plenty of substance. If they were arranged less tightly the tendrils would hang loosely with reduced impact.

This is a large project and time consuming, but it is well worth the effort as it is a highly original item.

Design Ideas

✤ The design can be made into a tiara or a crown and can be adapted easily to any size.

✤ Although the tendrils have not been designed to stand up straight, this could be achieved by working with a thicker grade of wire.

✤ The tendrils have been made in three graduating lengths, but again this could be adjusted or the whole tiara could be created using the smaller tendrils if a less dramatic effect is desired.

Equipment
2mm (US0, UK14) knitting needles
Scissors/wire cutters

Materials
Two strands of 0.2mm (AWG 32, SWG 36) wire, both about 197ft (60m)
$\frac{1}{8}$in (3mm) glass pearl beads and $\frac{5}{32}$in (4mm) Bicone Swarovski crystal beads, approximately 110 of each
Tiara band

This tiara is knitted using two strands of thin wire to give it strength without compromising the ability to make the small, tight stitches required to give the finished item its form. It has a knitted band which is then folded back on itself and stitched into place. The stitching is tightened to gather the band, which helps provide support and also acts as a hem through which the tiara base is threaded.

The beads are dropped into place at the end of each tendril and three beads are used on the central section. The beads are inserted alternately, which means they must be threaded alternately onto the wire before starting.

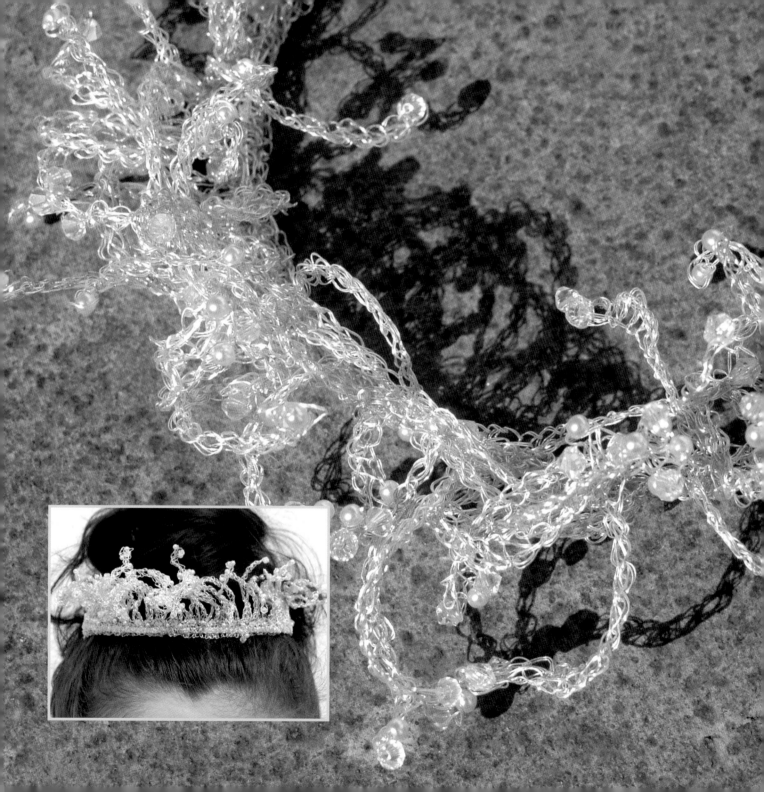

First side

1 Thread the beads alternately onto two strands of wire.

2 Working with the two strands of wire together, cast on 11 stitches using the traditional cast-on.

3 Drop a bead into place before starting the cast-off then cast off ten stitches, leaving one stitch on the knitting needle **ⓐ**.

4 Repeat 21 times giving 22 tendrils in total and leaving 22 stitches on the knitting needle **ⓑ**.

5 Repeat the above, casting on 14 stitches and casting off 13 stitches 22 times, to create a further 22 tendrils. You should have 44 stitches on the needle.

Centre section

6 Working with two strands of wire together, cast on 17 stitches using the traditional cast-on.

7 Cast on a further three stitches, dropping a bead into place each time **ⓒ**.

8 Knit one stitch, slip the next three stitches from the needle and gently pull into a chain, knit the next stitch on the left-hand needle and then proceed to cast off in the normal fashion, casting off 16 stitches and leaving one stitch on the knitting needle **ⓓ**.

9 Repeat 21 times, giving 22 tendrils in total and leaving 66 stitches on the knitting needle.

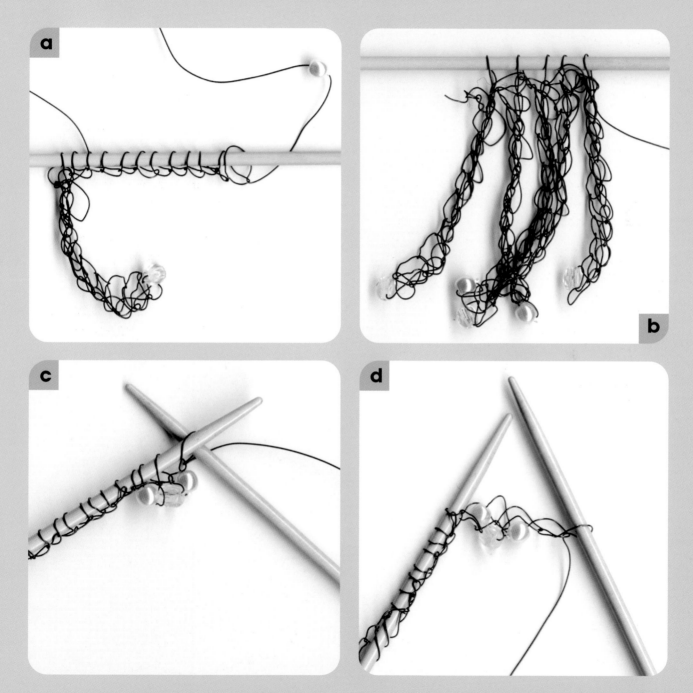

Knitted Tendrils Tiara

Second side

10 Make a further 22 tendrils as described in **Step 5**.

11 Make the remaining 22 tendrils as in **Steps 2–4**. There should now be 110 stitches on the needle.

12 Knit one row over these 110 stitches, dropping a bead into place in every other stitch **e**.

13 Purl one row then continue in stocking stitch for another four rows.

14 Cast off, either using the traditional method or by drawing the wire through the stitches to secure.

15 Stitch the band in half so that the cast-off end of the band is being stitched to the beaded row **f**. Keep the stitches tight to draw the work in.

16 Thread the tiara band through the 'hem' of the work.

17 Fashion the tendrils into shape, curling the central ones around a pencil to give definition as required.

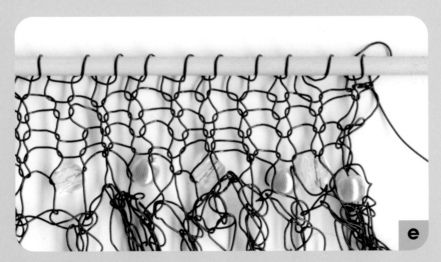

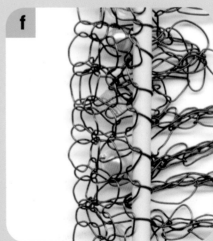

The same technique was applied to create this unusual neckpiece. The collar was made a little longer and, of course, didn't have a tiara band fitted. This demonstrates how, with a little imagination, the projects can be adapted to make many different and interesting items.

Knitted Tendrils Tiara

PROJECT PREPARATION

MATERIALS

Many hours will go into
making some of the projects in
this book, and therefore it makes sense
to buy the best-quality materials you can.
It would be a shame, for instance, to make a
piece of jewellery using good-quality beads
but a poor-quality wire that quickly tarnishes.
That said, while practising, mistakes are
likely to be made, so for your first few
attempts it is perhaps wise to go for
the less expensive options.

Metals

Historically, precious metals have been the material of choice when making jewellery. Gold jewellery has been found in many of the great archeological sites across the globe. Today there is a wider range of materials available to us. However, it is still metal that is at the heart of jewellery-making.

CHOICE OF METAL

Two key factors in choosing metal wire for jewellery-making are the visual appeal and the usability. The visual aspect is highly personal and, with the large variety of colours available in craft wires, there is huge pallet to chose from. With regard to usability and function, there are a few more aspects to consider.

Hard and soft metals

When knitting and crocheting with metal wire it is imperative that the metal is soft. When people talk about soft or hard metal they are referring to the ability of the metal to be bent and shaped before it cracks or breaks. A good example of this is that of a paperclip. When a paperclip is straightened a couple of times it will bend back into its original shape without difficulty. However, if you continue this exercise, eventually it will snap along the point where it has been repeatedly stressed. This is where the metal has become 'work-hardened', making it brittle. This can also be demonstrated with copper wire. Bend a piece in half and then straighten it. Repeat the process several times and eventually it too will

snap at the point that has been stressed, although you will find that it does not occur as quickly as it does with the steel paperclip.

A soft metal wire will bend and allow itself to be shaped. A hard metal will remain rigid and break. Soft metals, such as copper, silver and gold, can be manipulated into shape while they are soft and then hardened by a hammer to stiffen into place.

Wires that are most appropriate to knit and crochet with are soft wires that remain malleable despite bending and twisting. Although they will become work-hardened and brittle after much manipulation, they will retain their ease of shaping whilst knitting or crocheting (although if repeatedly knitted and unpicked they will snap, so if an area needs to be unpicked it is best to re-knit or crochet it with new wire).

The principle of soft and work-hardened metal is useful to bear in mind when designing and creating wire jewellery. When designing an item that bends or has movement, it is important to ensure that this movement is spread over a wide area and not specifically targeted at a single spot that will come under too much stress.

Silver and gold

Silver and gold are suitable for knitting and crocheting with. While silver- or gold-plated copper wire offers a cost-effective alternative, there is always the possibility that the silver or gold will wear away or become damaged during working, thus exposing the copper. Gold-filled wire has a thicker gold layer than gold-plated wire and can offer a good solution.

When working with silver there are two grades that are commonly available: sterling, which is 92.5% silver and 7.25% other metals, and fine silver, which is over 99% pure. If possible, it is best to work with fine silver which, besides being extremely soft and malleable, is also much less likely to tarnish than sterling.

Don't be put off by the price of precious metal sold by the metre; the cost of buying small units of anything is always proportionately more expensive, as it allows for the additional time taken in preparing the order. Buying silver 'bulk' within a larger reel will be much more cost-effective.

Craft or art wire

Craft wire is copper wire with a coloured coating. This wire is malleable and easy to use. It is also low-cost, presenting an ideal material to practise with. Craft wire is available in a range of colours and thicknesses. As with all coated wires, it is important that you don't damage the coating, otherwise the copper or metal underneath will become exposed and may tarnish.

Note: When working for a while with copper or sterling silver wire, it is not unusual to find that the metal has given the skin a slight 'patina' where the metal has come into contact. This affects some people more than others. A simple wash with soap and water will clean it away.

HOW TO BUY WIRE – REEL VERSUS COIL

Wire can be bought in a variety of ways, by weight or length, reel or coil. Traditionally, precious metals are sold by weight, and if purchased from a bullion dealer the price is fixed at the current day's rate. However, if buying precious wires from other suppliers, the price is generally fixed and the supplier will either sell wire by weight or length.

Larger quantities of wire are sold on reels, similar to cotton on a cotton reel. Smaller lengths of wire are sold coiled. Wherever possible, use reels of wire rather than coils. A coil of wire will inevitably 'spring' open and become tangled at a remarkable speed. A coil of unraveling wire is not a pleasant sight! It is nigh on impossible to straighten out effectively, often getting kinks and bends that simply cannot be removed. The process of untangling wire can also start to work-harden it. If a coil is the only option, then gently wind it round an old reel or cone. Failing that, keep the coil tied together, releasing only a metre at a time to ensure there are no tangles.

Wire is readily available from craft shops, jewellery suppliers and bullion dealers, as well as from specialist suppliers (see listings on pages 176–177 at the back of this book).

WIRE GAUGES

Wire is available in a number of thicknesses or gauges, ranging from the extremely thin to the very thick. The best wires to knit or crochet with are those that are thin enough to work without being so thin that they break.

Throughout the book, wire has been referred to in metric, plus the AWG (American Wire Gauge) and SWG (Standard Wire Gauge) standards. There are also wire conversion charts on page 174. A slight variation in wire size will not make a difference to these projects, so if in doubt ask the supplier for the size nearest to that which is quoted.

WIRE QUANTITIES

The lengths of wires quoted within the projects are approximate and will vary from reader to reader.

Wire is likely to be bought in a $1\frac{3}{4}$oz (50g) reel and this will go a long way. For instance, a $1\frac{3}{4}$oz (50g) reel of 0.2mm (AWG 32, SWG 36) wire contains 574ft (175m), which is enough to complete many of the projects in this book.

Materials

Glass Beads and Gemstones

The inclusion of glass beads and gemstones presents an ideal opportunity to completely customize a piece of jewellery. An item made with glass beads will look quite different if made up with gemstones, and vice versa. The choice of bead or gemstone is entirely individual, and factors such as the visual appeal, how the finished item feels to the touch, colours, and so on, all need to be taken into account.

There are no hard-and-fast rules to be followed when working with beads and gemstones, but there are a few points to bear in mind.

Smaller beads and stones ($\frac{1}{16}$–$\frac{1}{4}$in/2mm–6mm) are the best size to use with finer wires. Larger beads can be incorporated, but could prove too heavy for the wire or 'overpower' the intricate feel of a piece of knitted or crocheted jewellery. Smaller beads will show more of the stitch, sitting within the work, while larger beads will appear to sit on top of it. Larger beads work well with thicker wires; for instance, an item worked in thick wire is complemented by the chunky feel of large beads (up to $\frac{5}{8}$in/16mm), where small beads might get 'lost'. Small beads when used with thicker wires can also slide around the stitch, losing the uniform effect. Of course, this could be an interesting feature and developed as part of the design.

Beads that are used in jewellery are most commonly manufactured from glass and are available in a vast array of shapes, sizes and colours. As well as glass beads, cut-crystal beads are available. These are often high-quality crystal and are ideal for use in fine pieces of jewellery.

Beads can be bought either by number or by weight, depending on the supplier and the nature of the beads sold.

Gemstones are very often thought of in connection with high-quality items of jewellery, but semi-precious and ordinary gemstones are available in bead form and can offer an exciting alternative to glass beads.

Gemstone beads are sold in a variety of styles, some calibrated and cut into uniform shapes and others 'tumble polished' and supplied as gemstone chip beads. The choice again is personal. Gemstone tumblechip beads have been used throughout this book. They are readily available in a wide range of stones and are a cost-effective way to buy the amount of gemstone beads required for some of the projects. Because the tumblechip beads are not

calibrated, they are of different diameters and can vary in size between $\frac{1}{16}$in and $\frac{3}{8}$in (2mm and 10mm) or more. The supplier will be able to give an indication of approximately how many gemstone beads there are to a strand or by weight unit if asked. Therefore, within the projects an approximate number of stones or beads required has been given and not a weight or number of strands so as to take into account the vast difference in bead size.

HANDY HINTS

Keep a look out for suppliers who offer a 'lucky dip' mixture of beads in a good weight, for example 35oz (1kg), as this can present an ideal opportunity to purchase a wide range of beads at a reasonable cost.

The process of making beads, both glass and gemstone, is a dusty one and therefore you will not only notice dust falling from inside the hole of the beads but also a dusty deposit on the outside. When the item of jewellery has been finished it will benefit from being soaked in hot water with a spot of detergent, rubbed over with a soft cloth and then rinsed and left somewhere warm to dry. This will give a sparkle to the beads and to the finished piece.

When purchasing gemstone beads of value it is worth ensuring they are bought from a 'reputable' source, and that if they have been colour enhanced or treated then it is clearly stated.

141

Findings

'Findings' is the collective name for the fittings and fastenings that are used when making jewellery. It includes the items which are added to a piece of work to complete it into the finished article, such as a brooch fitting, ear wire or a necklace fastening.

Findings can be made from most metals, and are widely available in both precious metals and in base metals from jewellers' supplies' shops, craft shops and bead suppliers. While much of the choice in metal is down to personal preference, it makes sense to buy top-quality findings, which not only hold the work securely, but also complement the quality of workmanship. It would be a shame after lavishing care and attention on producing a beautiful piece of jewellery to diminish the final effect by using cheap findings that may tarnish or break.

It is, of course, possible to make your own findings, so as to create a piece of jewellery that is entirely individual. However, the projects within this book have all been made using readily available findings.

HANDY HINT
Keep a look out in junk shops and jumble sales, as items of broken jewellery can often be found. Fittings and fastenings can be 'recycled' to bring an additional unique touch to your piece. The photograph shown top right on the facing page, for instance, is a vintage clasp that has been renovated with beads to match the cuff.

JUMP RINGS

The humble jump ring is found in many items of jewellery. It is the link between the item of work and the fitting, so a jump ring will be used to fasten, for instance, a drop to an ear wire to make an earring.

The standard jump ring is made from wire that is bent into a ring. When purchased, the jump ring will be twisted slightly to leave the ring open. When the ring is in place it is twisted together and should give a tight and secure finish. It is best to use heavyweight jump rings if possible, and whilst there are many different sizes available, $\frac{3}{16}$in (5mm) is a useful, all-purpose size.

There is one drawback when using standard jump rings with fine wire, and that is that the wire can often slip through the opening, no matter how tightly it appears to be shut. There are two alternatives to a jump ring that will help with this. One is a 'split ring', which works on the same principle as a key ring, and the other is a locking jump ring, which clicks together permanently, offering a solder-free way of securing a jump ring closed. Neither of these have an open join, which means that the wire cannot slip out.

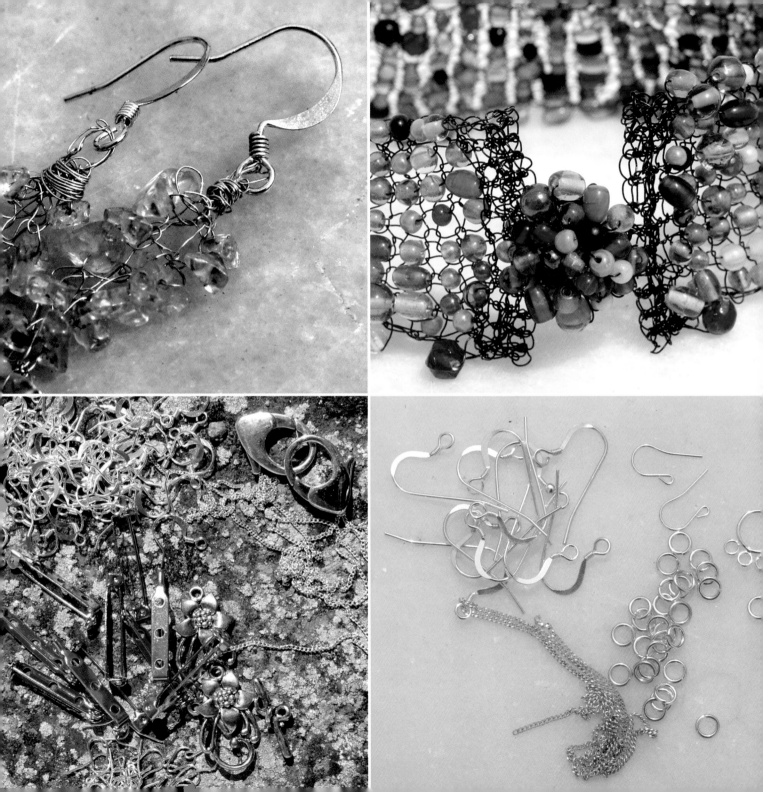

FASTENINGS

Fastenings are the method by which necklaces and bracelets are fastened together. There are many different types, the most popular being variations on the bolt ring and T-bar fastenings. Again, these are made in most metals and are widely available. Other types include hook-and-eye and multi-row clasps that are ideal for use with chokers.

When deciding what type of fastening to use there are a number of aspects to take into account; for instance, the overall 'feel' of a piece – would a delicate fastening look out of place on a chunky necklace? Also, practicality: a fancy, intricate fastening might be totally impractical to fasten onto oneself.

Fastenings often get forgotten about at the back of a neckpiece. However, they present the opportunity to add additional personality and a unique aspect to a piece. How about a vintage fastener from an old string of beads or a 'feature' clasp worn to the front of the neckpiece?

EAR WIRES

An ear wire or post is the part of the earring that is actually worn in the ear. It is essential, therefore, to only use fittings made from metal that is suitable for use as earrings (ideally hypoallergenic, silver or gold).

Ear wires are available in different sizes and styles, 'fish hooks' being the most common. Other types include safety ear wires that hook closed at the back, and these are good for use with 'precious' earring drops.

Ear posts are studs that have a ring fitted which will allow the earring drop to be fastened via a jump ring. These are held in place with butterfly clips.

Non-pierced fittings are available, and these are generally ear screws or ear clips. They are fastened to the earring drop, again using a jump ring.

Whilst the earring fittings mentioned above are the most commonly used, other types are available; ear hoops, for instance, which can provide an interesting and unusual way to wear earrings.

The ear wire or ear post is usually connected to the earring drop by a jump ring or, as seen in some of the projects in this book, through an integral part of the design.

BROOCH PINS

Brooch pins are fixed to the back of a piece of work to allow it to be fastened to a garment. The brooch pins are usually complete units which can be stitched to the back of a piece of work, and normally have a roller catch that holds the pin securely. These pins are stitched through predrilled holes into the finished pieces of work using wire as needle and thread. This will hold the brooch firmly on the pin.

HANDY HINT
A bit of epoxy resin under the brooch pin as it is stitched will provide extra security.

CHAINS, NECKLETS AND CHOKERS

Chains, necklets, chokers, and the such like, can be bought ready-made to hang pendants from or to decorate in other ways. Chain is available in plated metals as well as silver and gold and can either be finished with fasteners or sold by the length for you to finish with your own style of fastener. There is a wealth of different types of chain available, and the final choice is down to personal preference and what best suits the particular piece of jewellery being made. The important feature to note is that the chain is robust enough to support the weight of the piece.

Necklets and chokers are available in metals or other materials, such as rubber, leather or silk. There is a huge variety, ranging from the simple to the more ornate. As well as ready-made necklets and chokers, items can be made using various materials. More exciting ways of presenting pendants and neckwear can also be explored; for instance, a light, lacy pendant will look stunning looped onto a piece of sheer ribbon.

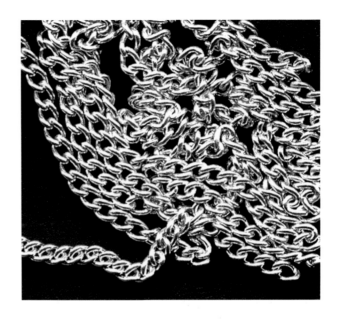

TIARA BANDS

Tiara bands hold the tiara in place on the head. These can be bought or made from wire. The key features to look out for with tiara bands are that they are light and comfortable to wear. Commercially available tiara bands have been used within this book, and most tiara bands can be adjusted to fit.

The bands are generally available in base and plated metals, either in a silver or gold colour. Their colour and appearance can be changed, however, by wrapping coloured wire or beads around them. The tiara is securely fastened to the base by wire.

EQUIPMENT

Many of the tools
required for the projects
in this book can be bought
secondhand or otherwise
acquired – borrow or ask nicely
if you can have cast-offs from
friends and family and an
extensive tool collection can
soon be gathered.

Hooks and Needles

Crochet hooks and knitting needles are the most important pieces of equipment required. Any crochet hook or knitting needle can be used, but it should be remembered that working with wire can be quite tough on needles, so it is best not to use an expensive set unless they have been bought specifically for this purpose. It's also worth keeping needles for use with metal separate from those used for working with yarns, in case any nicks appear in the needles.

Different-sized hooks and needles provide different effects. Small, thin needles and crochet hooks create tighter, denser forms compared to thicker ones, which will provide a more open or 'lacy' feel. Hook and needle sizes have been suggested throughout, but do feel free to experiment and see what difference working with a bigger and smaller sizes makes.

Old hooks and needles are fine; in fact, those from the attic, junk shops or granny's old workbasket, which nobody knows what to do with, offer a perfect, low-cost way to gather a range in different sizes. Failing that, both are widely available, and metal versions are not expensive to buy. Wooden ones are good for working with finer metals, but they soon get nicked and splintered with heavier grades of wire.

The UK and the US identify sizes differently, and of course there are still plenty of older hooks and needles around with the old imperial numbers. To avoid confusion, metric, US and old UK sizes are given throughout, plus there are charts on page 175.

Scissors and Wire Cutters

Another essential item required is a tool to cut wire. Traditionally, a metalsmith would use a set of wire cutters; however, as the wires used in these projects are of a fine gauge an pair of old scissors will work just as well. As with needles, if scissors are to be used then it is best that they become dedicated wire scissors.

A pair of proper wire cutters will ensure a clean edge each time the wire is cut, and are essential when cutting thicker wires. There are broadly two forms of wire cutter: side cutters, which operate the same way as scissors, or top cutters, which 'pinch' the wire. For the projects in this book, either will be fine. However, the side cutters are the easiest to work with.

148

Pliers

Pliers are required for the fixing of findings or fasteners to the finished pieces. It is possible to work with a single pair, but two sets make the job a lot easier. Any small pliers can be used, as long as they can be comfortably operated in one hand and the bed of the pliers is smooth so that they don't mark the metal. However, there are a number of types designed for different purposes.

SNIPE-NOSED

Snipe-nosed pliers have a relatively fine tip and look like two semicircles that are clamped together. They are multi-purpose pliers and are useful for holding small pieces of work. They are also available with a bent tip. You may find it helpful to own both types.

ROUND-NOSED

Round-nosed pliers are used to form wire into a ring. They are particularly useful for making jump rings, which are used throughout the book.

FLAT-NOSED

Flat-nosed pliers have two equal flat-bed tips that are usually about $\frac{3}{8}$in (10mm) in width. They are good all-purpose pliers.

Other Tools

There are other tools and equipment that may be useful but not necessary. These are as follows:

FILES

A fine file can be used to smooth any rough ends of wire. You should look for needle files, which are much smaller than the files found in most hardware stores.

WORKBOX

A workbox can be bought cheaply from Do-It-Yourself or hardware stores. The best ones to look out for are those with lots of different compartments, useful for storing materials and tools as well as work in progress. Failing this, plastic storage containers with tightly fitting lids are useful, particularly for storing beads and findings, which will seek every opportunity to throw themselves over the floor.

WORKBENCH

A jeweller's workbench is not essential but is certainly useful, particularly when working with precious metals and expensive beads. A series of trays on a kitchen table, or storage boxes with lids, will make perfectly adequate alternatives if working in an area that is not a dedicated work area, and will allow work in progress to be moved easily for storage.

MANNEQUIN OR DUMMY

A mannequin or tailor's dummy is very useful when designing items, as the jewellery can be tried against the dummy as work progresses through each stage. However, a mirror or willing volunteer will do as well.

LIGHT

Good light is essential, and can be supplemented with a specific craft light, an ordinary table light or perhaps a head torch. While a head torch may present the rest of the family with many hours of amusement, it will provide an effective way of giving additional directed light when required.

TECHNIQUES

There are a number of key
techniques that will allow you to
create all the projects within this
book, and these are detailed here.
There are no particular 'right' or 'wrong'
approaches, though, so if you are an
experienced knitter or crocheter
and have a preferred way of
working then this is fine.

Crochet Techniques

SLIP KNOT

The slip knot is the first stitch in crochet and knitting, and provides the loop from which the rest of the stitches are formed.

HANDY HINT
A slip knot in fibres, such as wool or string, can be pulled undone. Wire is less forgiving, though, and therefore rather than undo a slip knot it is best to discard that piece of wire and start again.

1 Take the short end of the wire in your left hand and the reel end in your right .

2 Using your right hand, twist the wire back on itself, making a loop over the short end **b**.

3 Draw the wire from the reel end through the loop to form another loop **c**. If working with yarn, this would then be drawn tight. However, with wire it is not possible to do this, and it is therefore important to ensure that the knot is neat, pulling it as tight as possible **d**.

HANDY HINT
Remember, wire cannot be repeatedly undone and re-knitted or crocheted, as it will become brittle and snap. It is therefore recommended that any unfamiliar steps are worked through as sample pieces. This will also serve to give an indication of tension and the size of work created with different needle/hook sizes and wire types.

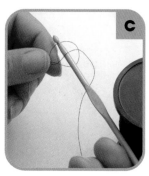

CHAIN

Making a crochet chain is very simple and builds on the slip knot.

1. With the slip knot on the hook in your right hand, hold the wire in your left **a**.

2. Wrap the wire around the hook from the back to the front **b** and pull this wrap through the loop of the slip knot to form a chain stitch **c**.

3. This is repeated, with each repeat counted as a chain stitch.

Note: When crocheting in rows, turning chains are required. This is one or more chains which bring the start of the new row to the necessary place. The individual projects detail the required number of turning chain/chains.

HANDY HINT
The first couple of stitches can be quite tough.
Hold tightly onto the base of the slip knot for
support using the left hand.

JOINING CHAIN

Chain is joined to form a chain ring or to join the chain within a piece of crochet or knitting. This is simply done by leaving the last crocheted chain on the hook.

1. Insert the hook through the stitch where the chain is to be joined, giving two loops on the needle **a**.

2. Wrap the wire around the hook as above **b** and pull through both loops, leaving a single loop on the crochet hook **c**.

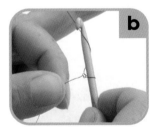

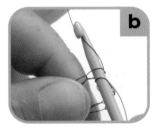

SINGLE CROCHET

Single crochet provides the densest mesh. While it gives a firm and attractive appearance, because of the density, it is also fairly difficult to work.

Single crochet is created into a foundation chain. Crochet one extra chain for turning, turn the chain so it is held in the left hand. The wire is at the rear of the work. With a bit of practice, Steps 2 and 3 will blend into a single motion.

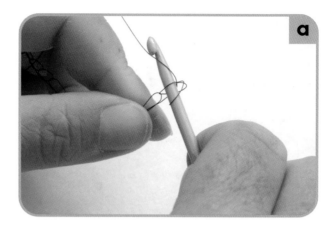

HANDY HINT
Single crochet can be substituted for any of the other stitches to create a firm piece of work. However, it is recommended to build up experience using double crochet, which has a slightly looser and open mesh, making it easier to work.

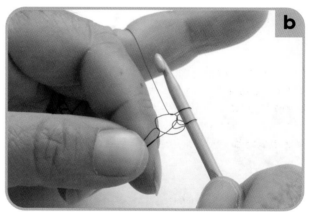

1 Insert the hook into one chain stitch **a** .

2 Catch the wire with the crochet hook and then draw it through the stitch, giving two loops on the needle **b** .

3 Draw the newly made loop (nearest the hook) through the other loop, leaving one loop on the hook **c** .

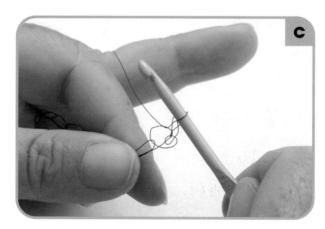

SLIP STITCH

This is the same as a single crochet, and is often used to join a round of crochet or to fix a chain into place.

DOUBLE CROCHET

The double crochet technique produces a regular and firm mesh, but it is less dense than one made by single crochet.

Double crochet is created into a foundation chain. Crochet one extra chain for turning and then turn the chain so it is held in the left hand. The wire is at the rear of the work.

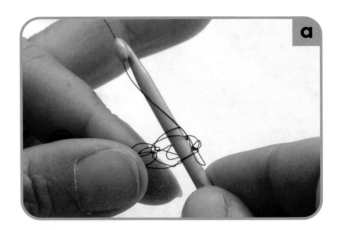

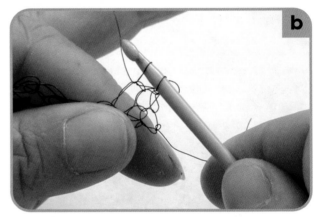

1 Insert the hook into one chain stitch **a**.

2 Catch the wire with the crochet hook and then draw it through the stitch, giving two loops on the needle **b**.

3 Wrap wire around the hook from the rear **c** to the front and draw the newly made loop through the other two loops, leaving a single loop on the hook **d**.

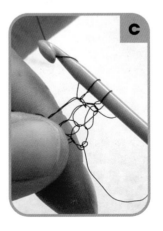

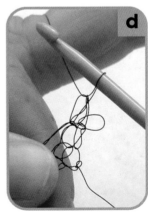

HANDY HINT
When crocheting mesh be careful not to 'crush' the work, as this can make it difficult to establish where the stitches are.

TREBLE CROCHET

Treble crochet builds on the process of the stitches already described, and when used in a mesh it gives a more open effect.

Treble crochet is created into a foundation chain, or in other projects into a chain ring. In either method, crochet two extra chains for turning, turn the work so that the wire is at the rear and the chain or loop is held in the left hand.

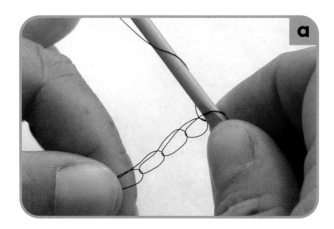

1 Wrap wire around the hook from rear to front **a** .

2 Insert the hook through the chain or through a loop. Catch the wire with the hook **b** .

3 Draw the hook and wire back through the stitch or loop. There will now be three loops on the crochet hook **c** .

4 Wrap wire around the hook from rear to front and draw through the first two loops on the hook. There will be two loops remaining **d** .

5 Wrap wire around the hook from rear to front. Draw through the remaining two stitches **e** .

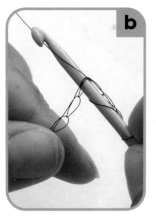

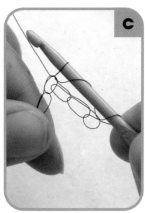

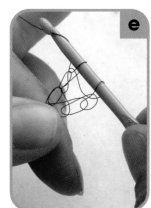

HANDY HINT
Keep a knitting needle nearby to 'poke' through any misshapen stitches. This will help to ensure the crochet hook goes through at the right place.

WORKING WITH BEADS

When crocheting with beads, the beads must first be strung onto the wire **a**. The beads will fall to the rear of the work; therefore every other row is crocheted with beads (otherwise beads will appear on both sides of the work). Naturally, the 'right' side will be the side with the beads showing.

Before the wire is wrapped round the hook or the hook is inserted into a stitch the bead is dropped into place **b**. The stitch is then formed in the normal way **c**.

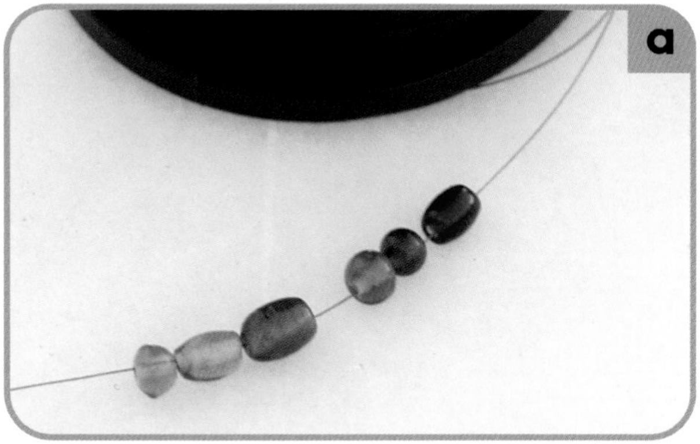

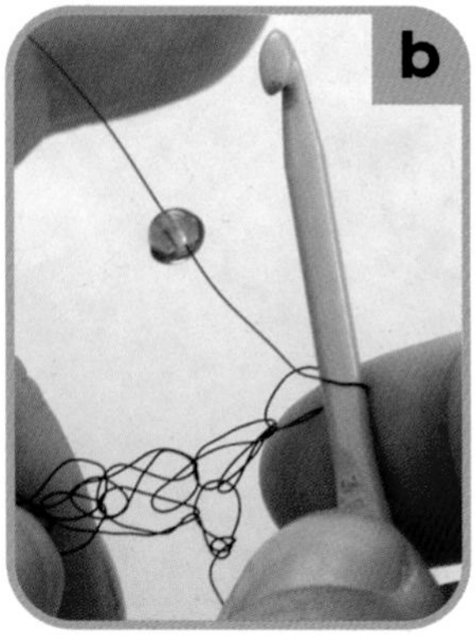

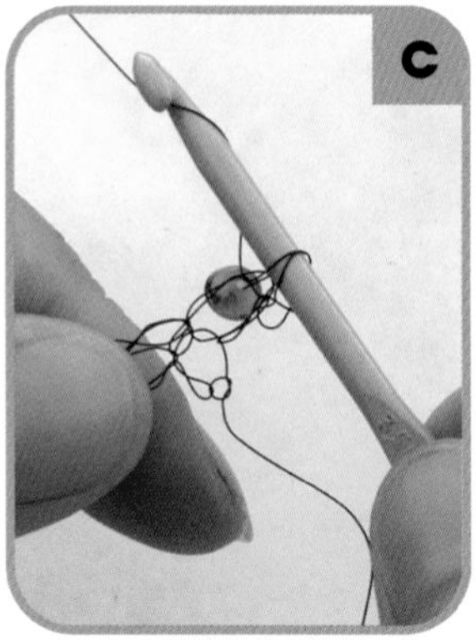

Design Ideas

- Try dropping beads into different places within a stitch to see the different effects, such as half way through the formation of a treble.
- Drop a bead into each row, giving a beaded effect on both sides, and use as earrings.

CROCHETED 'WHEELS'

Crocheting into a loop is the technique used to form 'wheels'. These can be worked in any crochet stitch.

To crochet a wheel, first a chain is made and joined to form a loop. The loop can be as big or as small as you like; however, a loop made from three or four chain stitches forms the base of the projects within the book. The number of stitches required will depend on the gauge of wire, size of hook and overall finished effect required.

Note: The wheel should lie flat when finished. Too many or too few stitches will cause the wheel to pull out of shape.

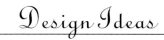

1 Make four chain stitches and join into a loop.

2 Make three chain (two for double crochet),
   treble crochet into the loop as follows: wrap wire
   around the hook **a**, put the hook into the centre
   of the loop rather than through a stitch **b**.

3 Take the wire and draw it back through the loop,
   giving three loops on the hook **c**.

4 Wrap wire around the hook and draw it through
   the next two stitches on the hook **d**.

5 Wrap wire around the hook and draw it through
   the remaining two stitches **e**, **f**.

6 Repeat around the loop to form a wheel.

7 The tail of the initial slip stitch can be wrapped
   around the chain loop, so that it is crocheted
   into the work and neatly finished.

HANDY HINT
*To make it easier to begin crocheting into the
loop, poke a knitting needle or pen tip through
the loop to shape it.*

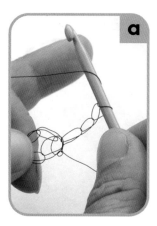
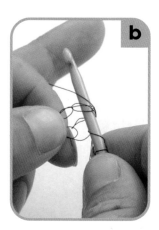
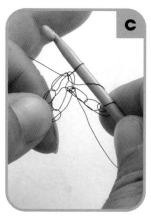
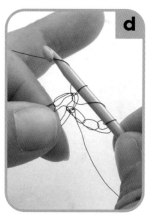
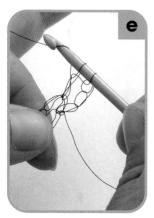
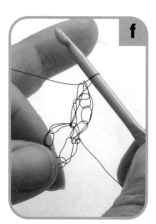

Knitting Techniques

The techniques for knitting with wire are much the same as knitting with yarn or fibre; however, wire has no 'give', and therefore it is best to knit rather loosely. The wire holds its shape well – much more so than fibre – and is less likely to unravel. In fact, it is unlikely to unravel even if it comes off the needle or if a stitch is dropped; instead, it will simply retain its shape.

When knitting with wire it is important not to bunch the work on the needle (i.e. squash the stitches together); instead, let it run smoothly up and down the needle. To experienced knitters this may feel strange, as they will be used to bunching the stitches up together for speed. A slow, methodical style of knitting is best with wire, so as to ensure that no parts of the work are put under stress and become work-hardened.

HANDY HINTS
The knitted wire can be pulled into shape after knitting – don't worry if it looks uneven up to then.

A knitting needle can be used to even out any stitches; for instance, to neaten the cast-on row.

CASTING ON WITH WIRE

Casting on with wire is different from the casting-on techniques with fibre insomuch as the main objective is to get a foundation set of loops onto a knitting needle, and the different features provided by different cast-on methods are less important. You need to ensure the stitches are loose – remember you are not knitting the ribbing of a sweater.

Two methods are given here: one is for a half-hitch cast-on, which is great for using with thicker wires, while the other is a traditional two-needle cast-on. This is a loose cast-on and may also be referred to as a lace cast-on. In this book it has been referred to as the 'traditional cast-on'.

Half-hitch cast on

A simple cast-on that is useful to know is basically a series of half hitches. This works particularly well when using a thicker grade of wire (0.4mm, AWG 26, SWG 27, and above), as the wire keeps its shape on the needle. However, it can be used with any wire, so experiment and decide which method suits you best.

1 Take one needle and the short end of the wire in your left hand, the reel end of the wire in your right hand. Twist the wire using the index finger of your right hand back on itself to form a loop 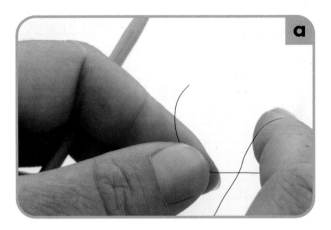 .

2 Put this loop onto the needle and pull tight 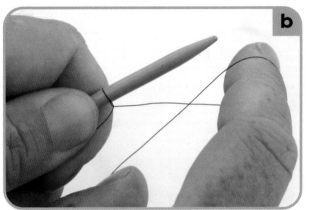 .

3 Repeat as many times as necessary 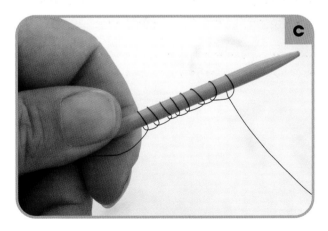 . Remember, wire has no give or stretch, so do not cast on too loosely. As a general rule, space the stitches the same distance apart as the needle width, i.e. space cast-on stitches about ¼in (6mm) apart on 6mm (US10, UK4) needles.

HANDY HINT
If you cannot achieve a loose-enough cast-on then try casting on with a larger size of needle.

Techniques

Two-needle/traditional cast-on

A more traditional cast-on is useful with finer wires, particularly those that are thin and flexible enough to act like fibre and yarn. Remember, don't pull the wire too tight.

1 Make a slip knot 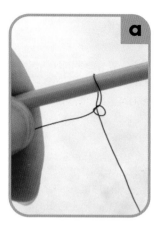.

2 With the slip knot on the left needle insert the right-hand needle under the stitch on the left needle .

3 Wind the wire around the needle in the right hand and then draw the loop under the right-hand needle , .

4 Put the loop that is on the right-hand needle onto the left needle, giving two stitches on the left-hand needle .

5 Repeat the process until the required number of stitches are on the left-hand needle .

KNIT

Many of the knitting patterns in this book are knitted in 'garter stitch' or 'knit' every row – this gives a highly textured surface which complements the wire. This is the standard knit stitch.

Note: The first row (in particular the first stitch) is tricky, but do persevere, as the following rows are easier.

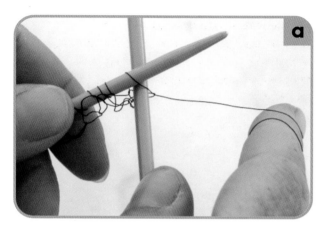

1. Holding the needle with the cast-on stitches in your left hand, the wire behind in your right hand, take the right-hand needle and insert it through the first stitch on the needle from front to back (in effect pushing it under the left-hand needle). The needles are now crossed at the top through the stitch **a**.

2. Wrap the wire around the needle in your right hand in an anticlockwise direction **b**.

3. Draw the needle in your right hand under the left-hand needle towards you, bringing with it the loop of wire just made **c**.

4. Slip the stitch you knitted into off the left-hand needle and repeat the process to the end of the row **d**.

5. To start the new row, simply turn the knitting and repeat with the desired stitch.

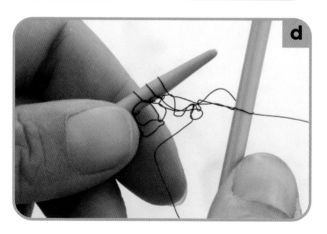

PURL

Purl stitch is similar to knit stitch, but the needle goes to the front of the knitting. By combining knit and purl alternately, stocking stitch or stockinette, is created, which has a smooth 'V' pattern on one side and a textured pattern on the other.

1. Holding the needle with the cast-on stitches in your left hand and the wire to the front of the work, take the right-hand needle and insert it into the first stitch on the needle from back to front – in effect pushing it under the left-hand needle. The needles are now crossed at the top through the stitch **a**.

2. Wrap the wire around the needle in your right hand in a clockwise direction **b**.

3. Draw the needle in your right hand away from you, under the left-hand needle, bringing with it the loop of wire just made **c**.

4. Slip the stitch you knitted into off the left-hand needle and repeat the process to the end of the row **d**.

5. To start the new row, simply turn the knitting and repeat with the desired stitch.

HANDY HINT
Wire is quite forgiving. If struggling, don't be afraid to give it a bit of a push or tug with your fingers.

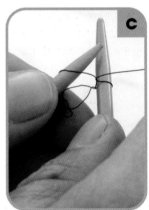

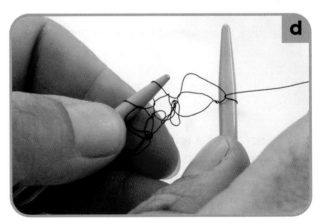

KNIT TWO TOGETHER

Knit two together is a standard way of decreasing. Simply insert the needle through the next two stitches on the needle and knit in the normal way , 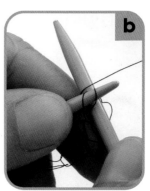.

CAST OFF

Casting off is the method used to hold the stitches in place and stop them from unravelling. With wire this is much less of an issue than it is with fibre or yarn, as the stitches will remain where they are when the needle is withdrawn. However, they will not withstand much handling without some form of securing or casting off. The options for securing these stitches can be as simple as drawing the wire through the last row to hold the stitches in place. A variation of this is to twist the wire around each stitch. Thicker-gauge wires will retain their shape best. With thinner-gauge wires a traditional cast-off can be used. The key here is to ensure as loose a cast-off as possible.

1 Loosely knit the first two stitches from the row .

2 Pass the first stitch (right-hand stitch) over the second to leave one stitch on the needle 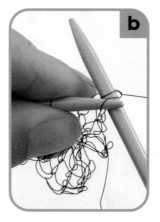.

3 Loosely knit the next stitch, giving two stitches on the needle, and repeat the process, taking the furthest stitch on the right over the other stitch. Continue until one stitch is left then draw the wire through this stitch .

KNITTING WITH BEADS

When knitting with beads, the beads should be strung onto the wire prior to starting to knit.

1 Prior to a stitch being formed, drop a bead into place **ⓐ**.

2 Knit the stitch as normal **ⓑ**.

BEADED CAST-ON/OFF

Beads can be dropped into the cast-on and cast-off stitches in the same way when using the traditional knitting cast-on and cast-off methods. After making your cast-on slip knot, drop a bead into place before making the next stitch. To cast off when using beads, knit the first stitch as in **Step 1** (left), then follow the directions on page 165, dropping a bead into place before each new knitted stitch.

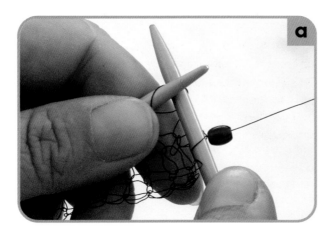

Common Techniques

TIDYING UP LOOSE ENDS

At the very least you will have two loose ends, at the start and the end of the work. It is important to secure these ends and to ensure they do not poke through the work and irritate the wearer.

One of the joys of working with beads is that the ends of wire can be wound around a bead a couple of times and snipped off close to it, or even tucked into the hole of the bead to keep them out of the way.

When there is no bead to wrap the wire end around, one of the best ways to tidy up any loose ends is to wrap the wire around a couple of stitches, tuck the end into the work and snip off closely. Alternatively, you could crochet or knit the end into the work, thus hiding it within the stitches. Long ends of wire can also be used to stitch findings onto the work or to stitch folded items together.

HANDY HINT
Sometimes it is useful to leave a long tail of wire to use in the finishing of the project; for instance, to stitch two pieces together.

JOINING WIRE

It may be necessary to join wire mid-project. To do this you simply work the two ends together for a number of stitches (two or three will be fine – remember it won't pull undone like wool or yarn) and tidy the ends up at the end of the work, as described.

If joining the wire in this way is going to be apparent (for instance with thicker wire) then it is possible to stop the old wire at one end of a row and start the next row with the new wire; the thicker wire will not slip or unravel. Once again, the ends can be tidied up as described.

PICKING UP STITCHES

Picking up stitches describes the technique of creating new working stitches onto an existing piece of work; for instance, stitches might be picked up at the ends of a collar to create a piece of supported mesh to fix the fastener to. Stitches can be picked up using knitting or crochet techniques.

For both knitting and crocheting it is recommended that the stitches are picked up using a crochet hook.

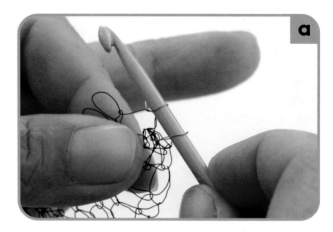

1 With the wire at the rear of the work, insert the hook at even spaces along the work where the stitches are to be picked up, so as to draw a loop to the front of the work **ⓐ**. This loop can either be worked as a crochet stitch or left on the hook to knit.

2 When the required number of stitches have been picked up, the loops are then transferred off the crochet hook and onto a knitting needle to continue working **ⓑ**.

THREADING BEADS

Threading or stringing beads onto wire doesn't require a needle, as the wire is thick enough to hold its own shape. That is the good news. The bad news is that this can be a tedious job, particularly when a lot of beads are needed. There are no 'quick fixes', so it is best to make yourself as comfortable as possible in a good, light workspace.

Some beads (in particular gemstone beads) come pre-strung and these can be taken straight from the temporary string onto the wire, which can offer quite a time saving.

Wind the threaded beads back around the reel and pull the wire through them as required.

HANDY HINT

Some of the projects require random threading of beads. Being 'random', though, is harder than it appears. To aid the process it can be useful to grade the beads into rough 'types' and then string alternately from each type, thus ensuring a degree of randomness!

FOLDING MESH

Knitted or crocheted wire can be flimsy. This can be a feature in its own right, giving a tactile element to the work. However, it also lends itself to being folded one or more times, which then brings a whole different dimension to the work, providing depth and detail.

Knitted or crocheted mesh can be folded either along the 'grain' of the work, which utilizes the natural fold in the metal along the rows (i.e. horizontally), or by increasing the metal in any place you wish.

When folding mesh along the row lines, both knitted and crocheted work has a 'right' place to fold. Feel the work and you will see what is meant. Knitting can be folded where you feel the looped edge. It will fold away from the loops. Crocheted mesh can be folded at any row, although gentle manipulation will help it fold along the row. To make a permanent fold, the work will need to be eased gently into place.

STITCHING/JOINING

Wire mesh can be stitched or joined together in a similar way to other related disciplines. For instance, layers of mesh can be stitched together using wire as both needle and thread. Two pieces of mesh can be joined by stitching or perhaps by a row of crochet.

It should also be noted that knitted and crocheted wire can, of course, be worked like any other metal, and therefore can be soldered, annealed or worked using any of the other metal-working techniques that might be applicable. Whilst these are not covered here, there is a wealth of information readily available on these techniques in books and on the Internet.

ATTACHING FINDINGS

Both the finding and the piece of work will largely determine the method of joining a finding to the finished piece. Generally, the key is to ensure that the finding is fixed in a secure manner with no loose ends to bother the wearer. Loose ends can be tucked into the work to keep them secure and avoid irritation.

Most findings are fixed using jump rings or are stitched in place (see Findings on pages 142–145).

When using jump rings it is important to ensure that the very thin wire does not slip through the opening of the jump ring, however tightly shut it appears to be. To avoid this, consider either using lockable jump rings, which snap permanently shut into position, or split rings. Both of these will ensure the wire doesn't pull through the jump ring.

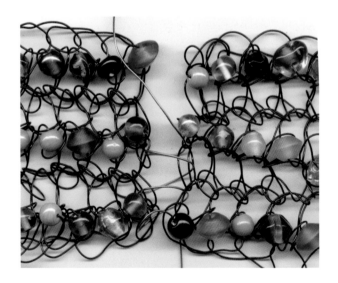

Wire Jewellery

Practice Exercises

If knitting or crocheting with wire is unfamiliar to you, it is recommended you work some sample pieces to familiarize yourself with the process.

The exercises detailed here are extremely useful, as they will allow you to assess the tension gained by working with different needle/hook sizes or grades and types of wires. They do not require much wire and only create small test pieces; however, the insight they give if you are knitting or crocheting with wire for the first time is invaluable.

HANDY HINT
Label each sample with the size of hook/needle and wire type used and keep for reference when planning other projects.

KNITTED MESH

Using small, medium and large needles, such as 2mm (US0, UK14), 4mm (US6, UK8) and 6mm (US10, UK4), cast on ten stitches and work ten rows of garter stitch (i.e. knit stitch every row), following the instructions on page 163, then ten rows of stocking stitch (knit one row, purl one row repeated). (See Purl, page 164.)

Measure the finished pieces and get a feel for the effect of the different-sized needles and the variation between garter and stocking stitch. Pull the squares into shape and feel how the stitches lock together. Try different cast-on methods (see pages 160–162) and note how important it is for a loose cast-on row. Experiment with cast-offs, i.e. traditional or threading wire through stitches (see page 165).

CROCHETED MESH

Using small, medium and large hooks, such as 2mm (USB-0, UK14), 4mm (USG-6, UK8) and 6mm (USJ-10, UK4), make a foundation chain of ten stitches (see page 154) then, following the instructions given on page 156, work ten rows in double crochet, followed by ten rows of treble crochet.

Measure the finished pieces to get a feel for the effects gained by using different-sized needles and different stitches.

CROCHETED WHEELS

Following the instructions given on page 158, create crocheted wheels with a range of different-sized hooks. Experiment by varying the number of stitches and also by 'pulling' the finished stitches to create a lacy effect. Record the gauge of wire used and the size of hook, as this will be useful when designing earrings using the technique on pages 34–37.

HANDY HINT
Repeat all the exercises using a thicker wire and get a feel for how working with wires of varying thickness changes the outcome.

Techniques

Conversions and Terms

WIRE CONVERSION CHARTS

There are a number of ways to measure wire, either by gauge or by diameter. The charts below show the approximate metric conversion of the American Wire Gauge (AWG) and the Standard Wire Gauge (SWG). If in doubt, please refer to your supplier who will be able to advise you on the nearest equivalent.

American Wire Gauge (AWG)	Equivalent in mm
33	0.18
32	0.2
31	0.22
30	0.25
29	0.29
28	0.32
27	0.36
26	0.4
25	0.45
24	0.51
23	0.57
22	0.64
21	0.72
20	0.81
19	0.91
18	1.02

Standard Wire Gauge (SWG)	Equivalent in mm
38	0.15
37	0.17
36	0.19/0.20
35	0.21
34	0.23
33	0.25
32	0.27
31	0.29
30	0.30/0.31
29	0.34
28	0.37
27	0.41
26	0.45
25	0.5
24	0.59
23	0.61
22	0.71
21	0.81
20	0.91
19	1.01
18	1.21

Note: The figures have been rounded and therefore may differ very slightly from equivalents provided in other tables.

KNITTING NEEDLE SIZES

Metric (mm)	US	Old UK
2	0	14
2.25	1	13
2.75	2	12
3	–	11
3.25	3	10
3.5	4	–
3.75	5	9
4	6	8
4.5	7	7
5	8	6
5.5	9	5
6	10	4
6.5	10.5	3
7	–	2
7.5	–	1
8	11	0
9	13	00
10	15	000

CROCHET HOOK SIZES

Metric (mm)	US	Old UK
10	P-15	000
9	N-13	00
8	L-11	0
7	K-10 1/2	2
6.5	10 1/4	3
6	J-10	4
5.5	I-9	5
5	H-8	6
4.5	7	7
4	G-6	8
3.75	F-5	9
3.5	E-4	9
3.25	D-3	10
2.75	C-2	12
2.25	B-1	13
2	B-0	14
1.75	6 steel	
1.5	8 steel	
1	11 steel	
0.75	12 steel	
0.60	14 steel	

UK/US TERMS

UK 'Double Crochet' = US 'Single Crochet'
UK 'Treble Crochet' = US 'Double Crochet'
UK 'Cast Off' = US 'Bind Off'
UK 'Miss' = US 'Skip'
UK 'Tension' = US 'Gauge'

Suppliers

Buying Online

Online auctions present an interesting way to seek out unusual products. They will often supply small quantities, too, with no minimum purchase required. However, when considering buying through an auction site remember 'buyer beware' and ensure that the seller has a good, reliable track record. Ask questions such as 'Is that wire silver or silver-plate?' and 'Are those gemstone beads colour enhanced?'.

Australia

A & E Metal Merchants
www.aemetal.com.au
Tel: +61 (2)8568 4200

Bead World International Pty Ltd
www.beadworld.com.au
Tel: +61 (7)5534 1333

Canada

Canada Beading Supply
www.canbead.com
Tel: +1 (613) 727 3886

Lacy and Co. Ltd.
www.lacytools.ca
Tel: +1 (416) 365 1375

Country Beads
www.countrybeads.com
Tel: +1 (613) 727 3886

UK

Scientific Wire Co.
www.wires.co.uk
Tel: +44 (0)208 505 0002

Cookson Precious Metals
www.cooksongold.com
Tel: +44 (0)121 200 2120

The Bead Shop (Nottingham) Ltd.
www.mailorder-beads.co.uk
tel: +44 (0)115 958 8899

PJ Minerals
www.beads.co.uk
Tel: +44 (0)170 457 5461

US

Rio Grande Albuquerque
www.riogrande.com
Tel: +1 (800) 545 6566

Metalliferous
www.metalliferous.com
Tel: +1 (888) 944 0909

Shipwreck Beads
www.shipwreckbeads.com
Tel: +1 (800) 950 4232

Fire Mountain Gems
www.firemountaingems.com
Tel: +1 (800) 423 2319

INDEX

To request a full catalogue of GMC titles, please contact:

GMC Publications Ltd., Castle Place, 166 High Street, Lewes, East Sussex BN7 1XU, United Kingdom

Tel: 01273 488005 Fax: 01273 402866

www.gmcbooks.com